FROM THE: CREATOR

photo: © '09 Billy Liner

You can't just make a magazine...

When I decided to end the web publication of Graveyard Girls and launch it into printed publication, I was told I'm doomed to fail, and ya can't just make a magazine. In this day and age when many publications are going to digital, I decided to take a digital publication to print. Many thought I was doing this backwards.

I'm not new to being told I can't do something. Back when Graveyard Girls originally started, I was told that it was a stupid idea, and nobody would care unless I was shooting nudes of the girls in cemeteries. Well, that was over 35 thousand shutter clicks and over 7 years ago.

In 2005 I took Graveyard Girls into being it's own web publication, instead of having it as a side feature of the original site. I again was told that it wouldn't work. 1 year later, the original site was abandoned, and Graveyard Girls was doing just fine.

Now I find myself entering 2010, still surrounded by skeptics, and still moving forward. I guess what a lot of people don't understand is I'm not afraid to gamble, not afraid of failure, and not afraid to shed my own blood to make great things happen.

Here it is folks. Issue 1 of Stiffmag is a reality. Once again I have done what just couldn't be done.

To all of you that believe in what I can do, I thank you. To the rest, get out of my way.

See you at the graveyard...

~Shane of the Dead

ON THE: INSIDE

In This Issue!

CREDITS:

• ON THE COVER: *"The Awakening"* by Mystic, with Graveyard Girl Amara

• Shane of the Dead - Creator/Publisher GraveyardGirls.net
• Dave Harlequin - Editor in Chief myspace.com/daveharlequin
• Mystic - Creative Dir./Photographer in Chief MysticManipulations.com
• Justin Kates - Stiff Photographer at Large TheJustinKates.com
• Billy Liner - Stiff Photographer at Large modelmayhem.com/linerb
• Immortal Image - Stiff Photographer at Large modelmayhem.com/immortalimage
• DayJaVUE - Contributing Photographer DaJaVUE.com
• Corey Daniels - Contributing Photographer modelmayhem.com/coreydaniels
• Larry Bradby - Contributing Photographer LarryBradbyPhotography.com
• Jimmy C of Luminous Impression - Contributing Photographer luminousimpression.com

• Torch - Sales Charlotte NC torch@graveyardgirls.net
• Dave Ward - Sales Greenville SC dave.ward@graveyardgirls.net

Stiffmag is a quarterly publication presented by graveyardgirls.net in association with singlecell.us. Please visit stiffmag.com for more information.

Greetings fellow horror fans!!

Welcome to the 1st issue of STIFF, a "by the people, for the people" alternative culture & entertainment magazine that chronicles how alternative culture helps shape the world we live in, as well as nearly every aspect of entertainment. We love all things dark & spooky... from movies, television and music, to modeling, technology and the fine arts. We also pride ourselves on giving the underground and independent scenes their much-deserved dues and credit, as well as maintain actual integrity in calling it as we see it from a real fan's perspective, rather than wasting your time with a bunch of sugar-coated, pseudo-reviews and out-of-context garbage you might find in some other magazines with similar themes.

To put things in perspective, horror has been a very big part of my life since I was a kid. Some of my fondest childhood memories involved sitting up way past my bedtime, watching such gems as "Monster-Vision", "Up All Night", "Tales From The Crypt" and "Alfred Hitchcock Presents" with my Dad (who was also a big horror fan). While most kids my age were watching Saturday Morning Cartoons, I was watching Midnight Movies. I'm willing to bet, if I dug around enough, I could still find my old toybox with my "Beetlejuice" and "Toxic Avenger" action figures.

When I first met Shane roughly 4 years ago, it was our shared love of all things horror that made us fast-friends. I started working with him on the old Graveyard Girls website & events. As our friendship continued to grow, so did our love for expanding our horizons, so naturally, when Shane approached me with the idea of doing a full-out magazine, with the offer to be editor-in-chief, I jumped all over it!

Now, many months and many sleepless nights later, despite everyone who either completely flaked on us, or just flat-out told us how stupid we were to invest so much time, money and effort into something that "couldn't be done", here we are! I know it's a very cliche thing to say, but all of our hard work has finally paid off.

I have a need in my heart to thank each & every person who contributed to getting this first issue off the ground. Everyone who submitted content, participated in and/or came out to and supported our fundraiser
events... or simply just helped spread the word. And a couple extra-special thank you's to Torch from SingleCell Productions, Mick from Ground Zero, Jynxx Midnite from Phantom Frequency Radio and of course Sandra Earley & Hollie Rode' for being so supportive and keeping me sane throughout all of this.

The magazine you're reading right now is living proof that with enough dedication, perseverance and undying (or maybe in this case, undead) love for something; that dreams can come true. To me, STIFF Magazine represents the continuing adventure of my life through my love for alternitive culture and all the joys such a truly great genre can bring. I sincerely hope that you, too, will find it in these pages.

Cheers!
Dave Harlequin - Editor in Chief

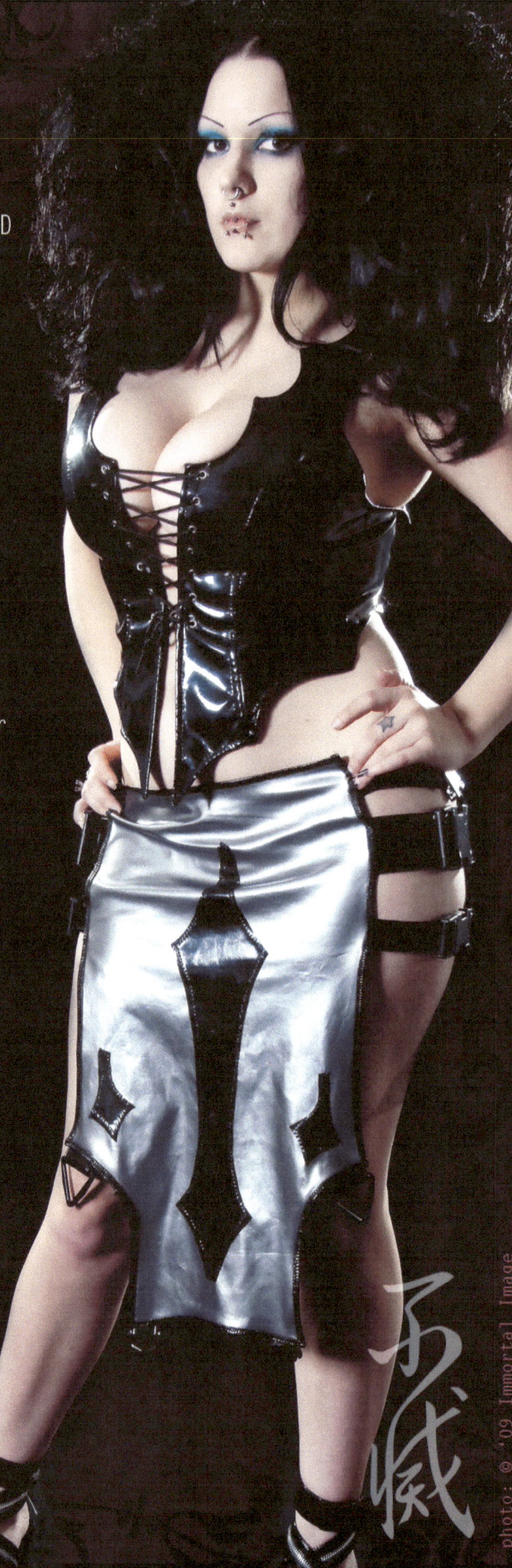

GRAVEYARDGIRL: HOLLEE HAZZARD

Come on kiddies, don't be afraid...
step right up and meet our Cyber
Goth Queen extraordinaire!

This professional dancer, model, performer
and owner of Hazzardous Hair, which is a
company that makes custom cyberlox, is all
about attitude, dancing and performing for
various artist and clubs all over the U.S.
for the past 7 years.

To know her is to love her... or if you
ever randomly see her on stage, dance floor
or photo shoot set, you will love her
before you know her!

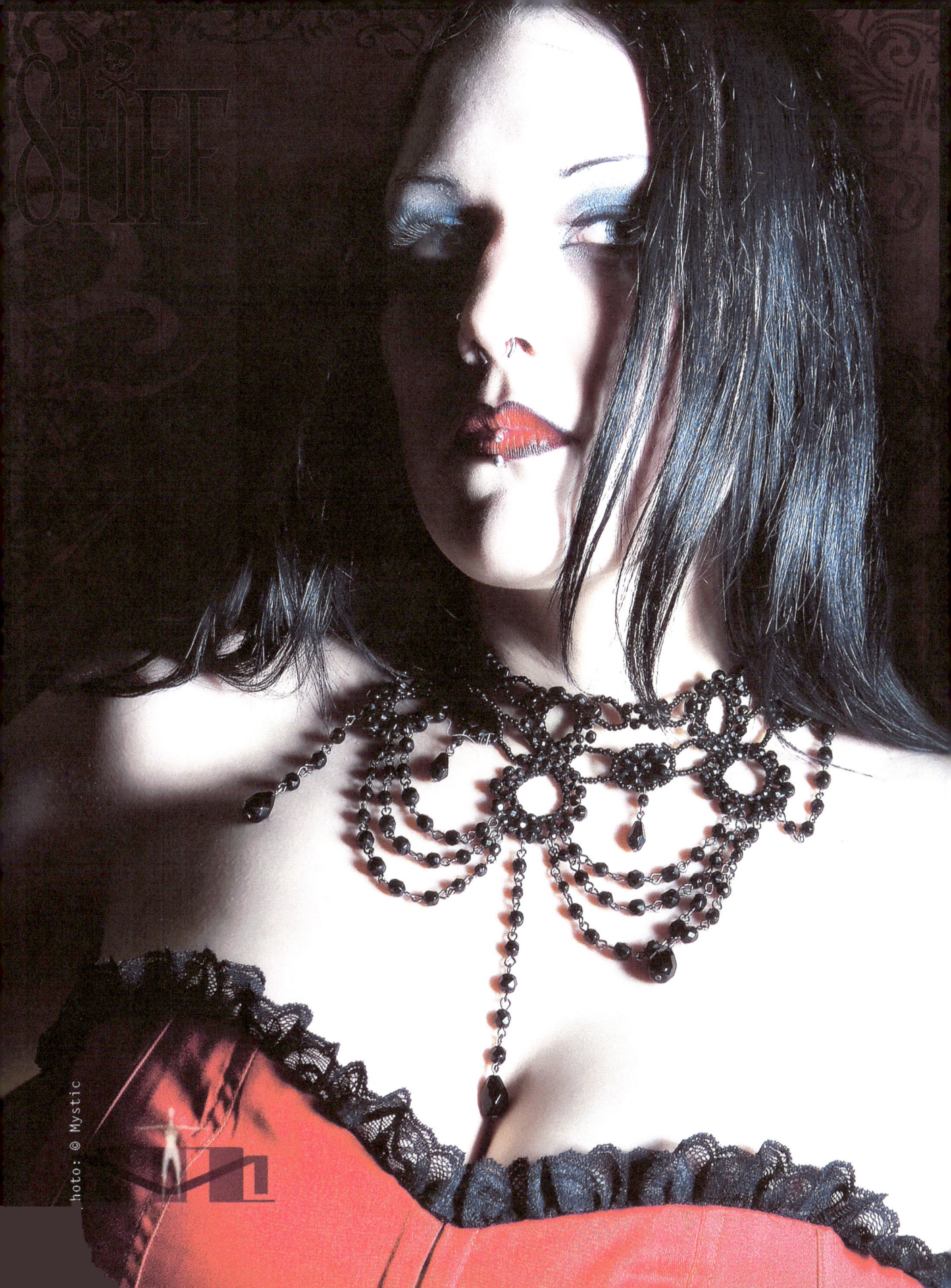

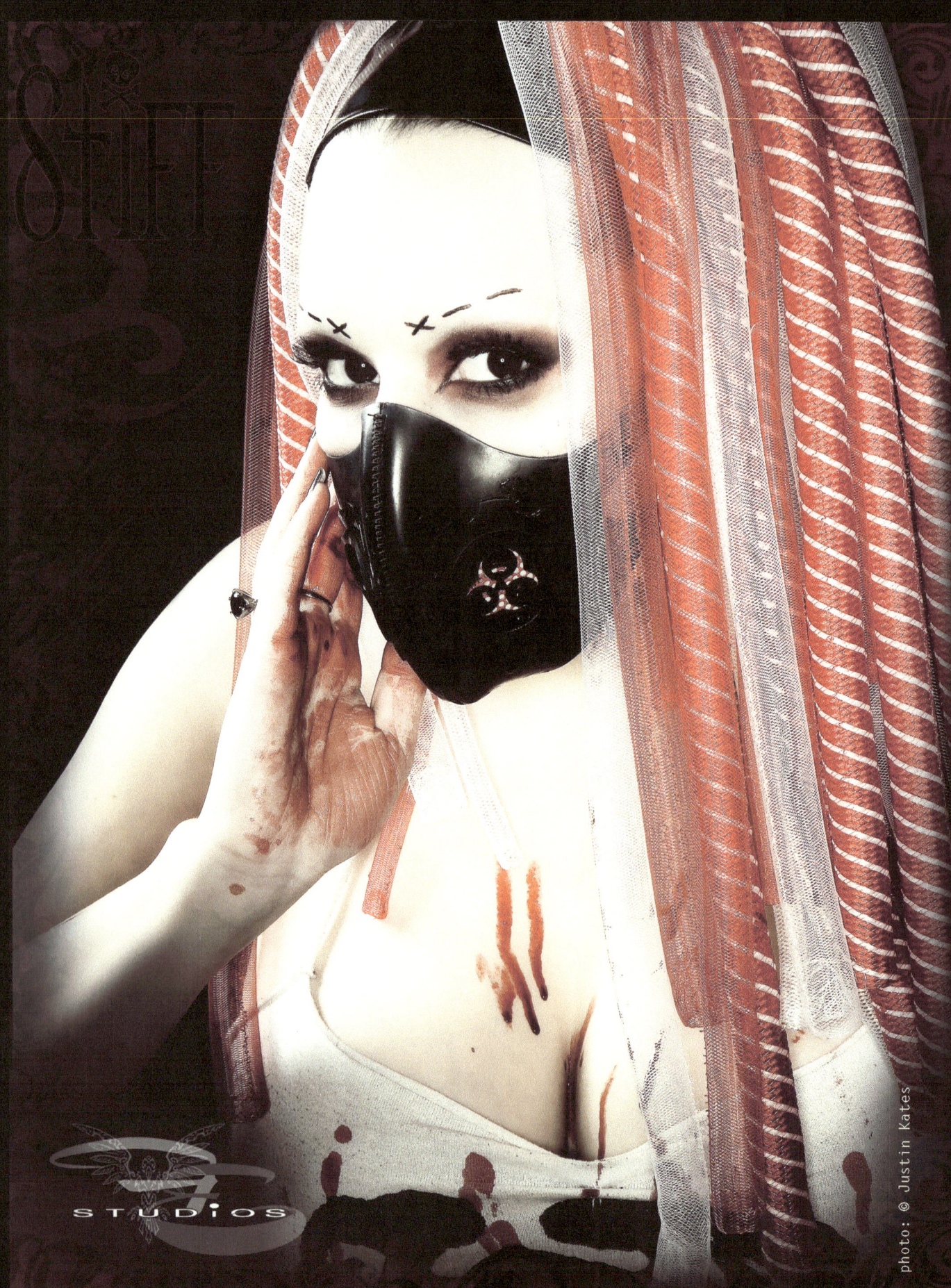

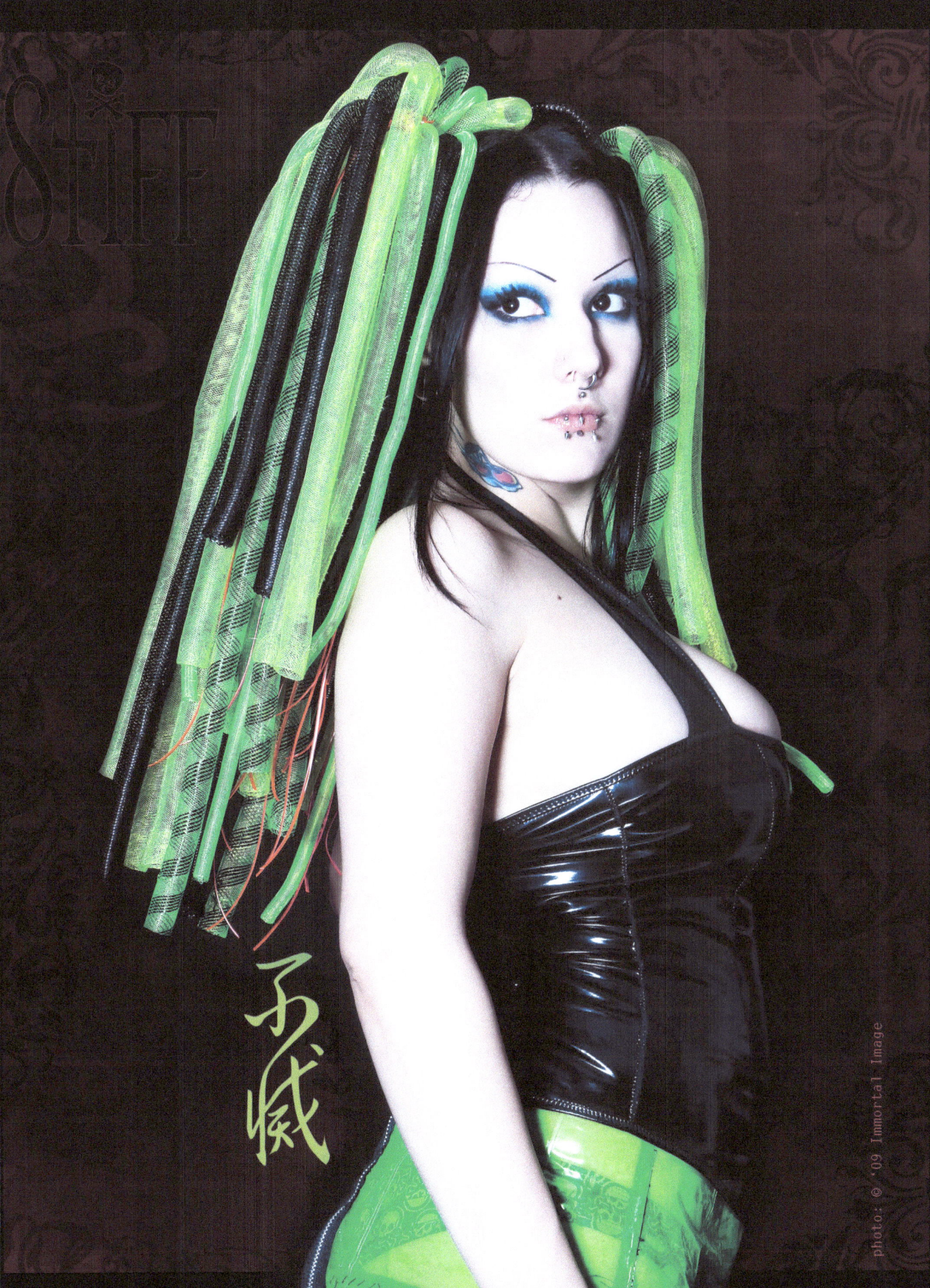

STIFF

一戒

photo: © '09 Immortal Image

www.myspace.com/bodybagsmusic

Charlotte, NC's horror-punk newcomers, The Body Bags, have already made quite an impact in such a very short time. Their debut full-length release "Modern Monsters", released February 14th, 2009 through Red Light Productions and produced by Ryan Zimmerman, is 16 tracks of pure, raw horrific goodness from start to finish.

In "Modern Monsters" The Body Bags have continued to raise the bar and set the standard for modern horror-punk, both by borrowing heavily from classic punk rock stylings and by adding a fresh, youthful almost nu-metal style to the very limited genre. Obviously, the album, much like the band itself, is anything but shy about their love for classic, retro & modern horror, which is very evident from the 2nd track entitled "Meet Me In The Graveyard", which starts off with the music from "Alfred Hitchcock Presents" and touts samples throughout the entire album from films such as "Army of Darkness", "Saw II", "Dawn of the Dead" and of course "The Lost Boys" which the entire last song of the album "Don't Drink With Vampires" is a complete homage to.

Kyle Monstrosity, lead vocalist of The Body Bags went on record for us in saying "it was a lot of fun recording Modern Monsters. I know that all of us got on each others nerves at some point in time, but we had a blast going in, messing around and doing what we love" he continued on to comment on their music in saying "every time we see a horror movie we like, we start getting ideas for songs and we honestly wouldn't be anything without our fans, they are the ones who drive us to write better music". The new record has without doubt, already gained the band quit a bit of notoriety, earning them shows alongside punk cult-favorites such as Blitzkid, The Graveyard Boulevard & Leftover Crack as well as punk rock-legends such as The Casualties and The Misfits.

The Body Bags have also earned international attention, with "Modern Monsters" being a featured album in Rue Morgue (issue #93) proving that our neighbors to the north have good taste as well!

Currently, The Body Bags are set to head back into the studio to record a brand new EP as well as begin work on their second full-length album. Unquestionably,

The Body Bags have a very bright future ahead of them, and horror-punk fans have much to look forward to!

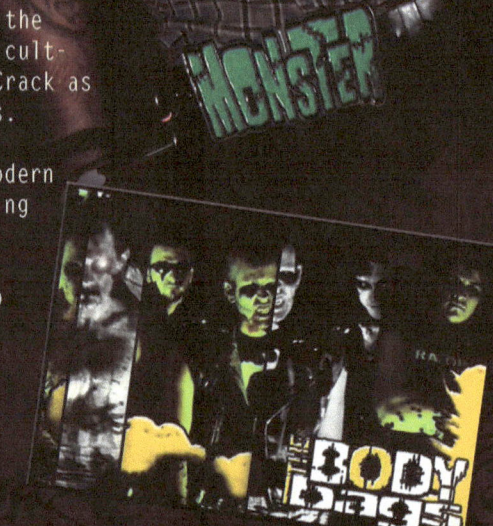

REVIEWS: MUSIC

ASSEMBLAGE 23: "COMPASS" ~Dave Harlequin

Seattle, Washington's Assemblage 23 return with their sixth full-lenth album "Compass" out on Metropolis/Accession Records. This new album is complete with all the usual aspects fans have come to know and love with the band, dark rhythmic blends of synthpop & modern electro dance, EBM influences and quality songs. "Compass" however adds a bit of a twist to the equation as the band introduces new influences such as electrohouse and post-punk as well as highly improved vocal talents by frontman Tom Shear.

The amount of quality tracks is bigger than on the previous album and with that it seems "Compass" is the best Assemblage 23 album since "Storm" and perhaps even since "Failure", but of course time will have to point that out. Whether it is the uptempo club tracks like 'Smoke', 'Collapse' and the single 'Spark' or ballads like 'Impermanence', 'How Can You Sleep?' or the splendid 'Leave This all Behind', the fun and energy is bursting from this electro album. Further recommended tracks are 'Alive', 'Greed' and 'Angels & Demons'. The limited edition of this album contains a second cd with a very accomplished KMFDM remix of the track 'Greed'. Highly recommended for anyone who likes a little bit of passion, depth and darkness with their dance music!

www.assemblage23.com   www.myspace.com/officialassemblage23

ANGELSPIT: "HIDEOUS AND PERFECT" ~Dave Harlequin~

Sydney Australia's Angelspit return with their third studio album "Hideous and Perfect", out now on Metropolis Records. While the new album feels very familiar to earlier releases with the usual blend of industrial, EBM and cyber-punk combined with very noticeable elements of horror as well as medical-fetish themes, it is still a bit of a departure from the sound many Angelspit fans are used to.

A couple songs show a rather drastic change from the standard aggressive Angelspit sound with the band utilizing slower more mellow beats with very serious dark lyrics, such as the song song "As It Is in Heaven". In many songs, the lyrics tend to revolve around money, greed and fascism, with song names like "Cold Hard Cash" and "Making Money" speaking out against such things as corporate lawsuits over college students breaching internet copyrights. So while the album still has the rebellious tone that previous Angelspit albums have, "Hideous and Perfect" goes much further on actually showing that message.

While the music is outstanding, the packaging alone is also well worth the price of admission. The album's photography showing the artistic side of the band, including ZooG and DestroyX in medically-inspired futuristic/cyberpunk-esque outfits really brings everything together. Definitely an album worth checking out!

www.angelspit.net

DETHKLOK: "DETHALBUM II" ~Dave Harlequin~

Dethklok, the fictional death metal band of the popular Adult Swim show "Metalocalypse" return with a vengeance with "Dethalbum II", the follow-up to "The Dethalbum", which for those keeping score is the highest charted death-metal album of all time on the Billboard Top 200.

Following in the footsteps of such acts as GWAR and Spinal Tap, Dethklok has made a huge impact on what is most often referred to as "comedy metal" with their hilarious and often ridiculous lyrical content and subject matter. Brendon Small and Gene Hoglan, the masterminds behind the fictional cartoon band, have seemingly tried to make a more serious album this time around. While many songs at times still written in comedic overtones, overall the album is much more technically sound and has a much more serious feel to it, at least in terms of death metal.

However, Metalocalypse fans have nothing to fear as the hilarity of Dethklok is still strong as well. Just from the title, "Laser Cannon Deth Sentence," it is apparent that comedy is at the forefront. "Cell-mates explode in front/Barbequed bone fragments bloodied face/Blistered skin" showcases some of the random, comedic lyrics that fans have fallen in love with.

Musically, "Dethalbum II" is in a class all of its own. Brendon Small, who graduated from the Berkley College of Music and recorded everything but the drums, makes sure to let everyone know that his talents go much farther than the realm of comedy and metal fandom. With Small's harsh yet vocals, intense riffs, blazing solos and incredible production value and the aggressive yet progressive and well-timed drums from long time metal journeyman Gene Hoglan, "Dethalbum II" stands as a big reminder that not taking oneself seriously doesn't always mean lack of real talent.

www.myspace.com/dethklok

Kiss - Sonic Boom / Alive 35 Tour ~Shane Trotter

Before going into this review, I have to say I have been a huge Kiss fan since I was in my teens. When I first heard there was a new studio album coming out, I knew I would end up buying it, and I did when the day came.

The Sonic Boom packaging is exactly what I expected of a Kiss album. With the guys going back to using the makeup during the 1990s, and continuing even after Ace Frehley and Peter Criss left the ranks again, the familiar iconic faces were easy to spot on the shelf. I picked up Sonic Boom on the day of release, and the $10 price tag was not bad for a release including 2 CDs and a DVD.

I have heard for months that Sonic Boom was to be a return to the Kiss roots, and I really did have high hopes for this album, but my expectations may have been too high. The albums this band released from 1974 to 1977 are all iconic and very strong albums, but I honestly do not hear classic Kiss in Sonic Boom. Recording the album may have been done in classic style, but it is just too clean and to well produced for me to really feel it.

If it were not for the over polished vibe I get from it, I may like it a lot better. Even the classics included on the bonus disk suffer this downfall, and honestly the only saving grace for me is the DVD included in the set. Simmons and Stanley need a reminder that rock and roll is supposed to be dirty.

After the disappointment of Sonic Boom came the decision of going to the live show, and I almost didn't go. Stadium events have really overpriced over the last few years, so I finally made the decision to get cheap seats at the back of the venue. This live show for me was really the saving grace, and delivered on the classic Kiss experience that Sonic Boom missed by a mile. Over half of the set list were tracks from the 1974-1975 studio albums, and the guys really seemed to have a good time on that stage. Only one track from Sonic Boom made it into the setlist.

The reality of Kiss is that they really are a live experience. The studio albums have never reflected what they bring to the stage, and that hasn't changed in 35 years.

www.kissonline.com

VNV NATION: "Of Faith Power & Glory" ~Dave Harlequin

Hamburg, Germany's VNV Nation returns with their 7th full-length album geared to light up goth/industrial dance floors and personal systems the world over. The latest release of FAITH, POWER, AND GLORY released June 23rd on Metropolis Records in the United States touts itself as the first CD release with the "lowest carbon footprint ever on a major label release". The new album is packaged in 100% fully reclaimed and recycled material, along with water based inks and glues, which leaves us wondering if green really is the new black.

VNV Nation have continued to raise the bar and set the standard for electronic, EBM, and Industrial acts the world over, and this album is certainly no exception. Although it could be said that this album doesn't exactly break any new ground except to head into slightly heavier territory on a couple of tracks, VNV Nation has always been able to blend brighter and darker (not to mention danceable) electronic sounds with very hard hitting, poetic and inspiring lyrics. Such a unique sound has earned them quite the strong reputation and a very dedicated fanbase the world over.

Unquestionably though, VNV Nation have produced one of their best albums to-date. It's a collection of accessible and nearly flawless electronic music that blends elements of Industrial, futurepop, dance and EBM for very resounding results.

www.vnvnation.com   www.myspace.com/vnvnation

INSANE CLOWN POSSE: "Bang! Pow! Boom!" ~Dave Harlequin

I know what you're thinking, and you're right. It is absolutely pointless to review any album by the Insane Clown Posse. The independent underground giants have made a career off being virtually critic-proof. Think about it. If you're not a fan, there's literally nothing anyone could say to convince you to check out this album and if you are a fan, there's literally nothing anyone could say to convince you not to check out this album. Of course, after several people asked us for an ICP review, we here at STIFF decided that regardless of everything just said, to do it anyway.

"Bang! Pow! Boom!" is the 11th studio album by the notorious horror-themed comedic hip-hop duo and is, believe it or not, their 2nd album to chart on the Billboard 200 "Top 10" (at number 4). The album also debuted at number 1 on the Billboard Top Independent Albums chart, selling 50,000 copies in its first week.

A major feat for any truly independent artist, especially the self-proclaimed (and widely agreed upon) "most hated band in the world".

The album is of course nothing particularly new or different, featuring the same silly songs, immature lyrics, subject matter revolving around murder, sex and generalized violence and an overall "dark carnival" theme that fans love and just about everyone else hates. As usual, the album also features several skits in which rednecks, pedophiles, husbands who abuse their wives etc. receive phone calls from band members Violent J and Shaggy 2 Dope.

"Bang! Pow! Boom!" is not for everyone, actually it's just for ICP fans (referred to as "Juggalos"), something the clowns take pride in with every album. So again if you're a fan, you're probably already going to give this album a listen, if you're not, then you probably won't. Either way, no one can deny the continued success of the Insane Clown Posse despite everything.

www.insaneclownposse.com   www.psychopathicrecords.com

MAKING THE BAND

So you think you've got what it takes to make it? Maybe you do. Most of you don't. Many of you reading this will try, and most will fail. It's not being negative. It's just reality, and your success or failure relies on the decisions you make as a band.

Some of you will consider the decision to start or join a band a personal hobby. Some of you will consider it to be following your dreams. Whatever your reason is, it all becomes a business move if you ever decide to play live shows, and you've got 2 huge decisions to make before you begin.

Many people begin their musical business ventures playing cover tunes. It really isn't a bad way to build your stage experience and obtain better gear, but for anyone wanting to make it big, covers are a death sentence. The sad reality is you become background music, which can just as easily be covered by a DJ, karaoke, or even a radio station. Nobody really cares.

I'm sure some of you out there reading this little article are absolutely livid right now that I've called you a failure, saying that you include your original tunes in a covers set. Do your fans request you to play your own material, or whatever radio hit is popular now? I'm sure you've all heard the term "play Freebird" at some point. No matter what the song request is, if it's not your song, your song isn't good enough.

The road to success is a hard one, and if you want to become big on your own tunes, you have to take the hard path to get it.

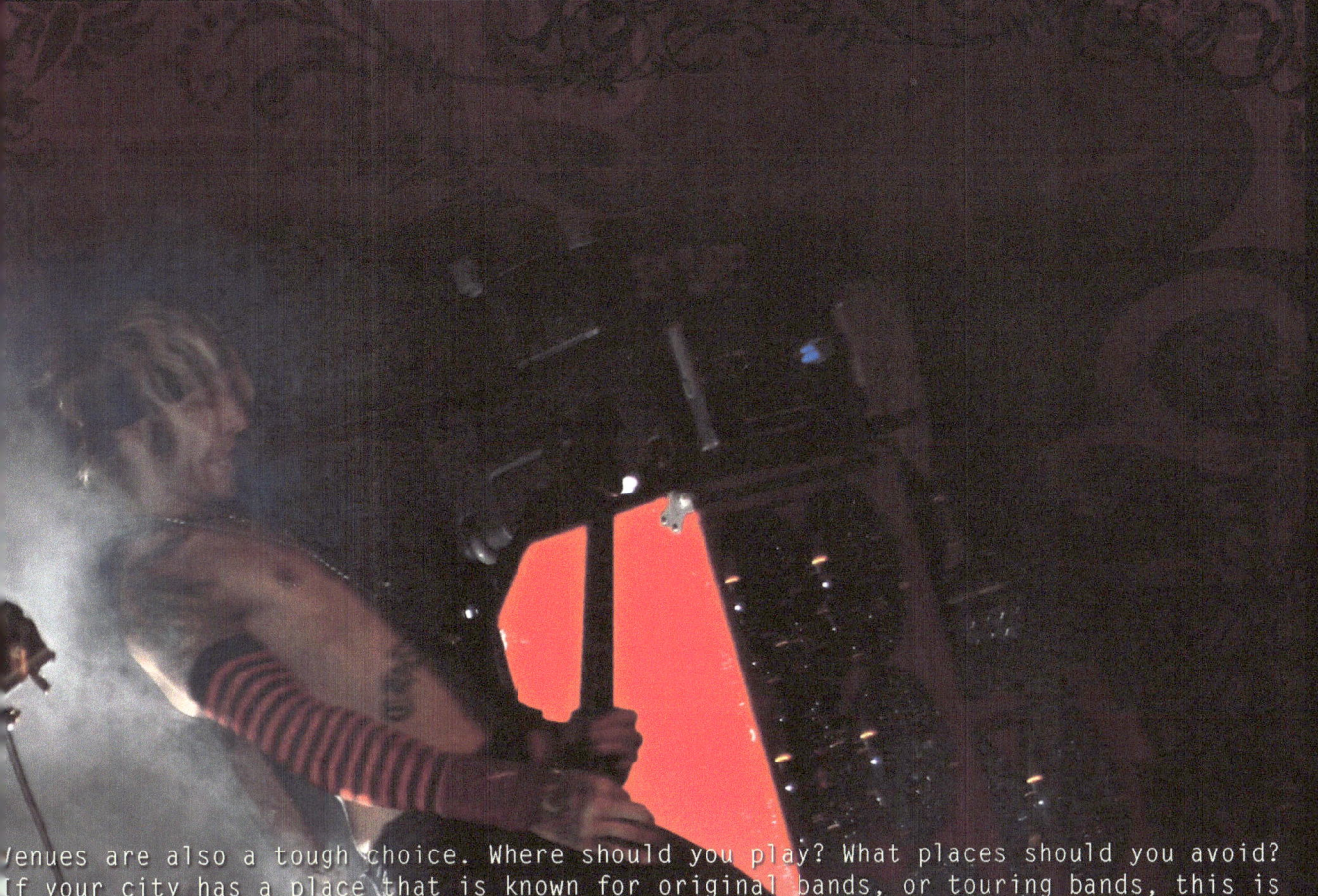

Venues are also a tough choice. Where should you play? What places should you avoid? If your city has a place that is known for original bands, or touring bands, this is where you need to play. Most people usually try to start at places with hot wings and beer specials, and while they are willing to give you a decent guarantee to play, they usually do not want original material. You also need to know if they are known more for music, or food and drink. If music is not the primary reason people go there, you do not want to establish yourself as one of their bands.

One easy way to tell if a venue is intended for original and touring acts is to look at the available seating. Is the place covered with tables? If there is seating available for more than 5% to 10% of the total capacity, this is not where you want to play. Standing room only is the ideal choice.

I'm sure some of you are now even more livid. There is reason for looking at the available seating, and if you have doubts, pay attention at your next show. How many people are up in front of the stage, and how many are in groups around tables trying to talk louder than you play?

Tables and seating are an instant guarantee that people will not pay attention to your show. They invite groups and conversation, and in turn damage your ability to entertain. If you need proof, see how many tables you see at a coliseum event, or at a movie theatre. None? Well why not?

Bands are really no different than any other form of a business. You do have to set your goals properly, you do have to work hard, and you do have to plan for success. Most of you will still fail, even if you do everything right to become famous. Don't worry. You can always go back to playing covers. Join us again next issue and we will cover wearing the uniform and keeping the day job.

~Shane Trotter

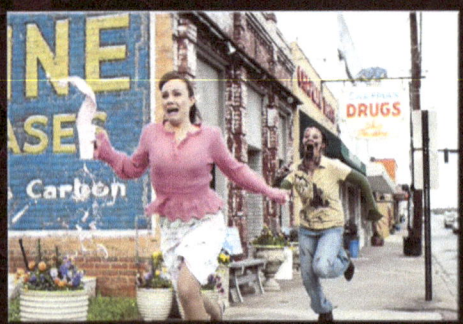

So yes, actually living through the zombie apocalypse doesn't sound all that amusing or entertaining... but I assure you, in Zombieland it absolutely is! This bloody, gruesome, and highly innovative horror-comedy revolves around four main characters; Tallahassee (Woody Harrelson: "Natural Born Killers"), Columbus (Jesse Eisenberg: "Adventureland"), Wichita (Emma Stone: "Superbad") and Little Rock (Abigail Breslin: "Little Miss Sunshine") who end up reluctantly working together to find a place where the "infection" hasn't spread. Along the way they encounter many random misadventures, conflicts, hilarious moments and of course, plenty of good old fashioned zombie-killing mayhem!

The characters, rather than using names, decide to refer to each other by where they're from so as to not become too attached to one another in the event of one of them "turning". This is of course all part of the "rules for surviving Zombieland" which Columbus had come up with. Columbus' list goes down to rule #31, with Tallahassee coining the final rule #32. I won't spoil the rules here, I'll simply say, if you don't already know the rules of surviving the zombie apocalypse, watch the movie! In addition to the rules, Zombieland also features other special segments such as the highly popular "zombie kill of the week".

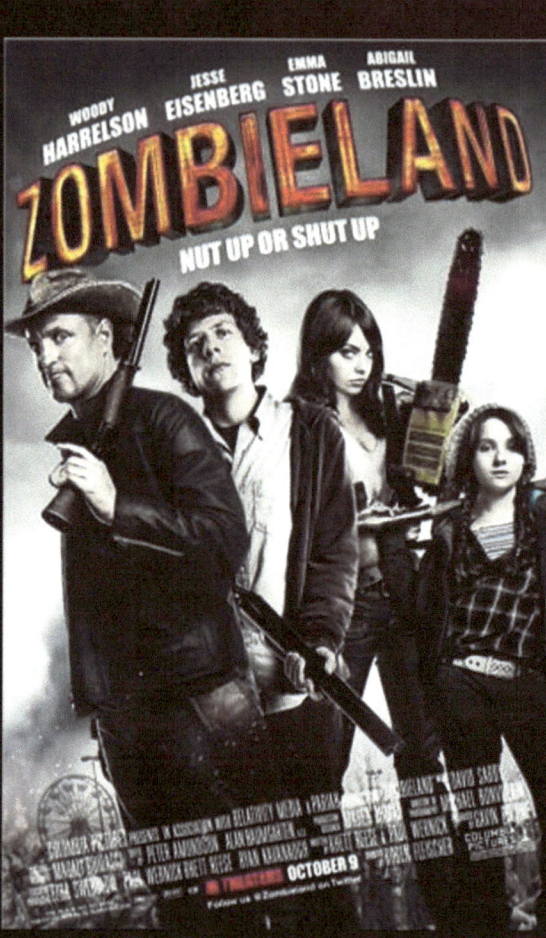

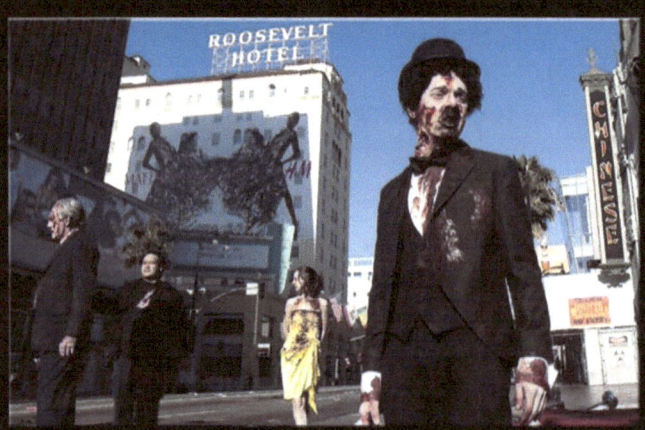

The basic plot of the film starts us off with Columbus, who is walking across what once was the states to get to Columbus, Ohio in order to reunite with his family when he comes across Tallahassee; as you can tell by the name he is driving to Tallahassee, Florida. They both agree to travel together, which is great for the fearful and paranoid Columbus because Tallahassee "sets the standard for zombie killing", but there is only one problem with Tallahassee; he is food motivated and stops at stores in hopes of finding the last Twinkie. While in search of a Twinkie, they come across two sisters Wichita and Little Rock who end up being experienced con-artists. As you probably guessed, they end up teaming up with the sisters, who are headed to an amusement park they have heard is "completely zombie free". As you also probably guessed, they're wrong, and thus the movie reaches it's finale with one last showdown against the legions of the undead.

Zombieland writers Rhett Reese and Paul Wernick have already mentioned the possibility of a sequel after the film's huge (and admittedly surprising) success at the box office, revealing that they have plenty of ideas for the film, which was originally conceived as a TV series. Paul Wernick, according to sources, went on record saying "The cast is very open to a sequel", though sources also tell us "this is dependent on the studio and the movie's performance – not the cast." Given the obvious success of the film however, I'd have to make my prediction for a yes.

As of this time there is no official date for a DVD release, though it is projected for late-January or early-February of 2010 and is highly rumored to be packed full of plenty of really fun extras and if we're lucky, maybe a zombified easter-egg or two! I suppose we'll just have to wait and see.

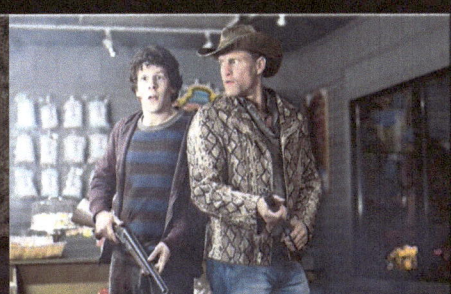

Overall, Zombieland is a highly entertaining, over the top hilarious splatterfest with an excellent cast (including a very special cameo from none other than Bill Murray), fantastic special effects, and of course, plenty of action, which will leave you wanting to watch it again and again!

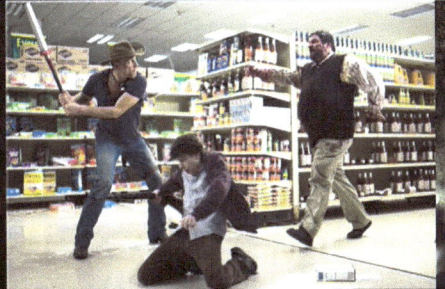
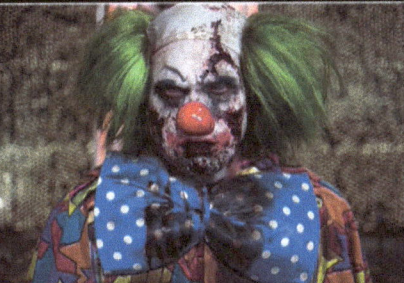

I personally loved it and easily give it 5 Scars!

- Dave Harlequin

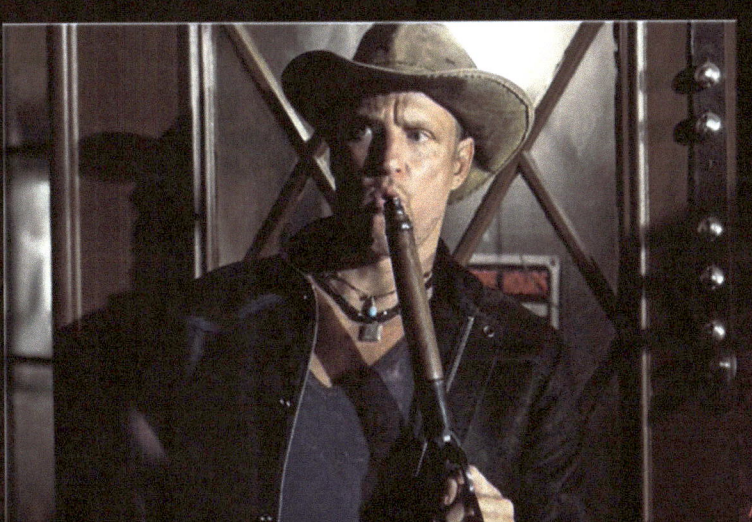
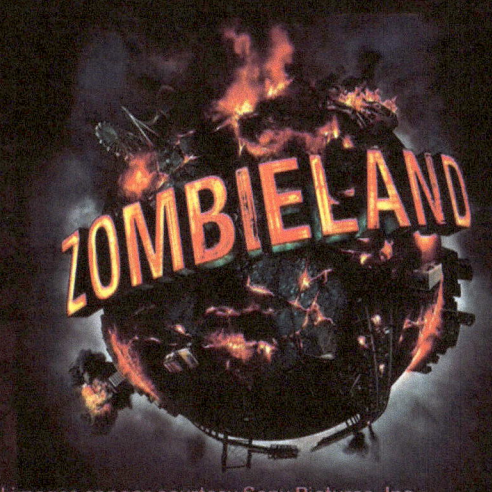

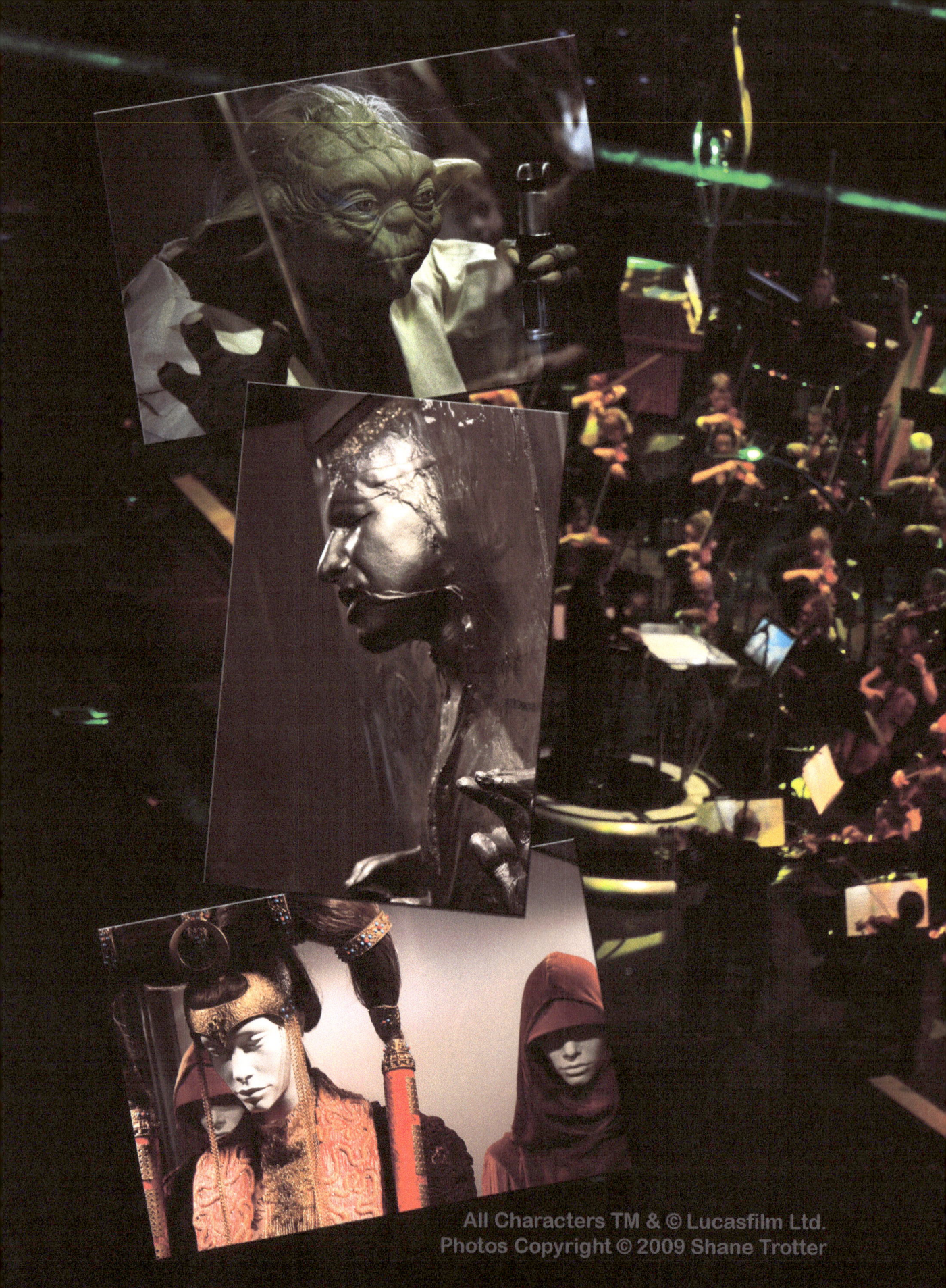

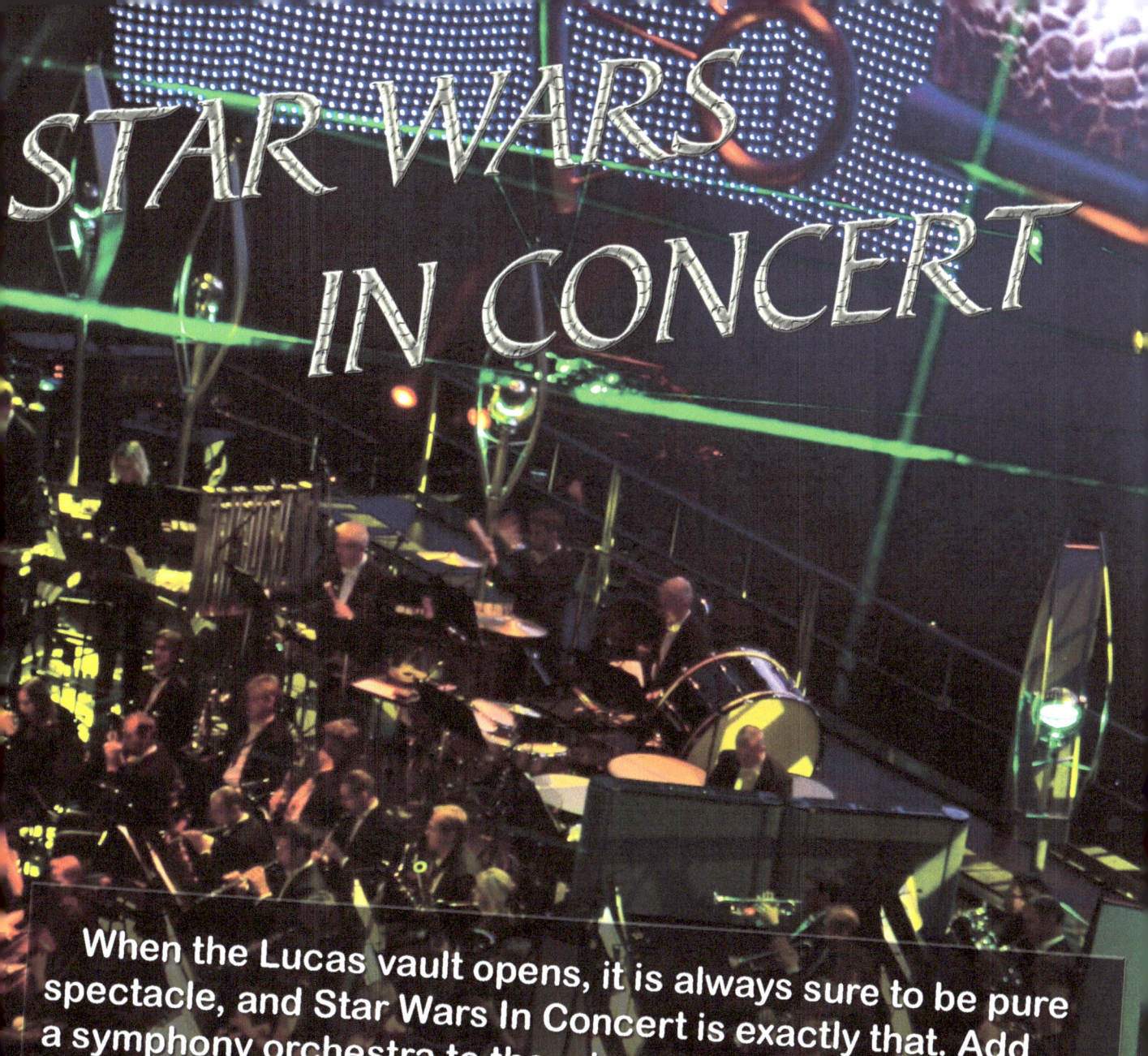

STAR WARS IN CONCERT

When the Lucas vault opens, it is always sure to be pure spectacle, and Star Wars In Concert is exactly that. Add a symphony orchestra to the mix, with the movie props and film clips, and you've got yourself a visual experience sure to satisfy.

Anthony Daniels, the actor behind the world famous droid C-3PO is your narrator in this trip into Star Wars film history, and the film scores all sound exactly as you would expect, but that's not all. The whole experience becomes complete with lazer effects, pyrotechnics, and humor for the fanboys all over the world.

Pretty Things Peepshow
December 2009
Spartanburg SC

STiFF MAG™

Photo: © '09 Billy Liner

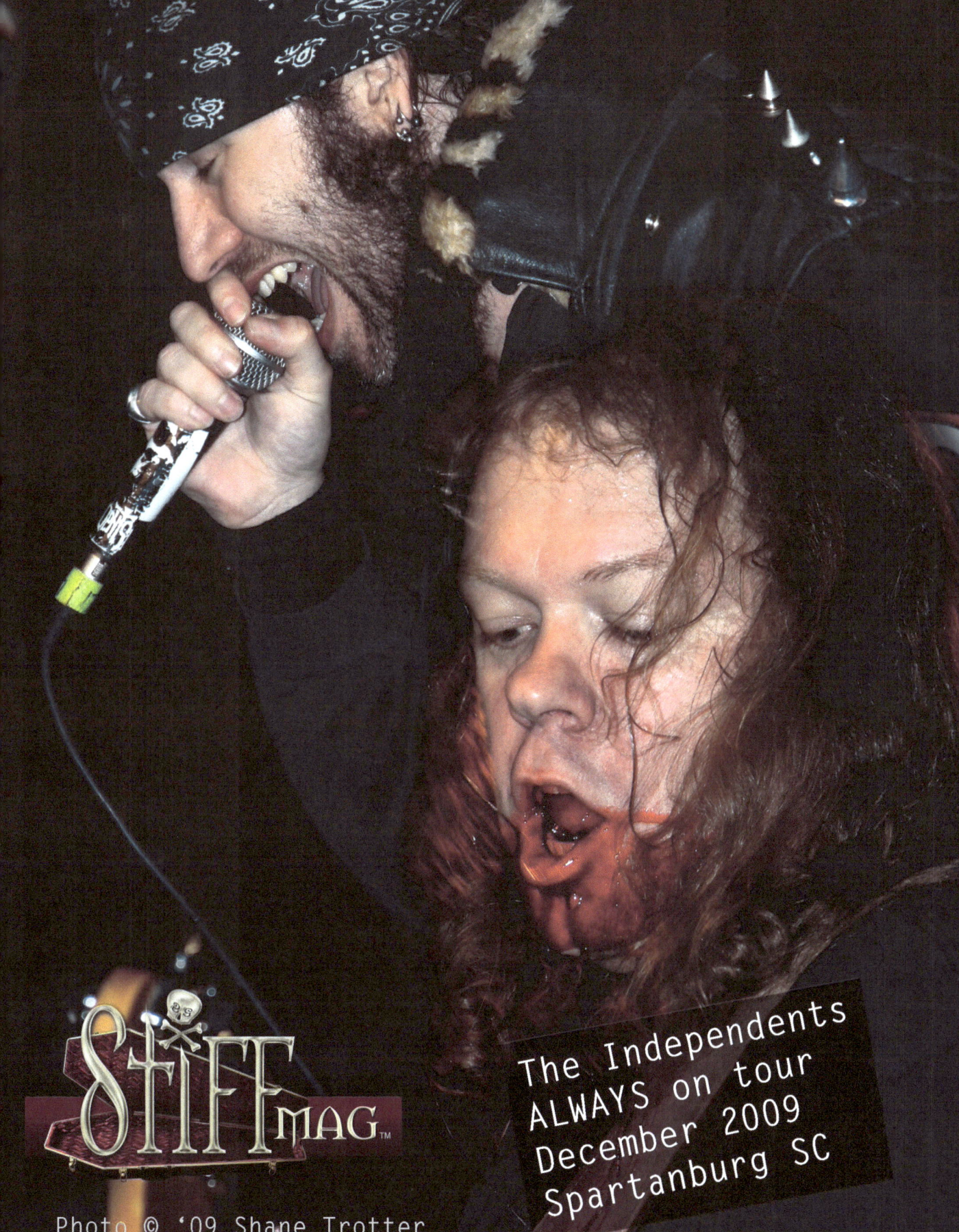

STIFF MAG™

Photo © '09 Shane Trotter

The Independents
ALWAYS on tour
December 2009
Spartanburg SC

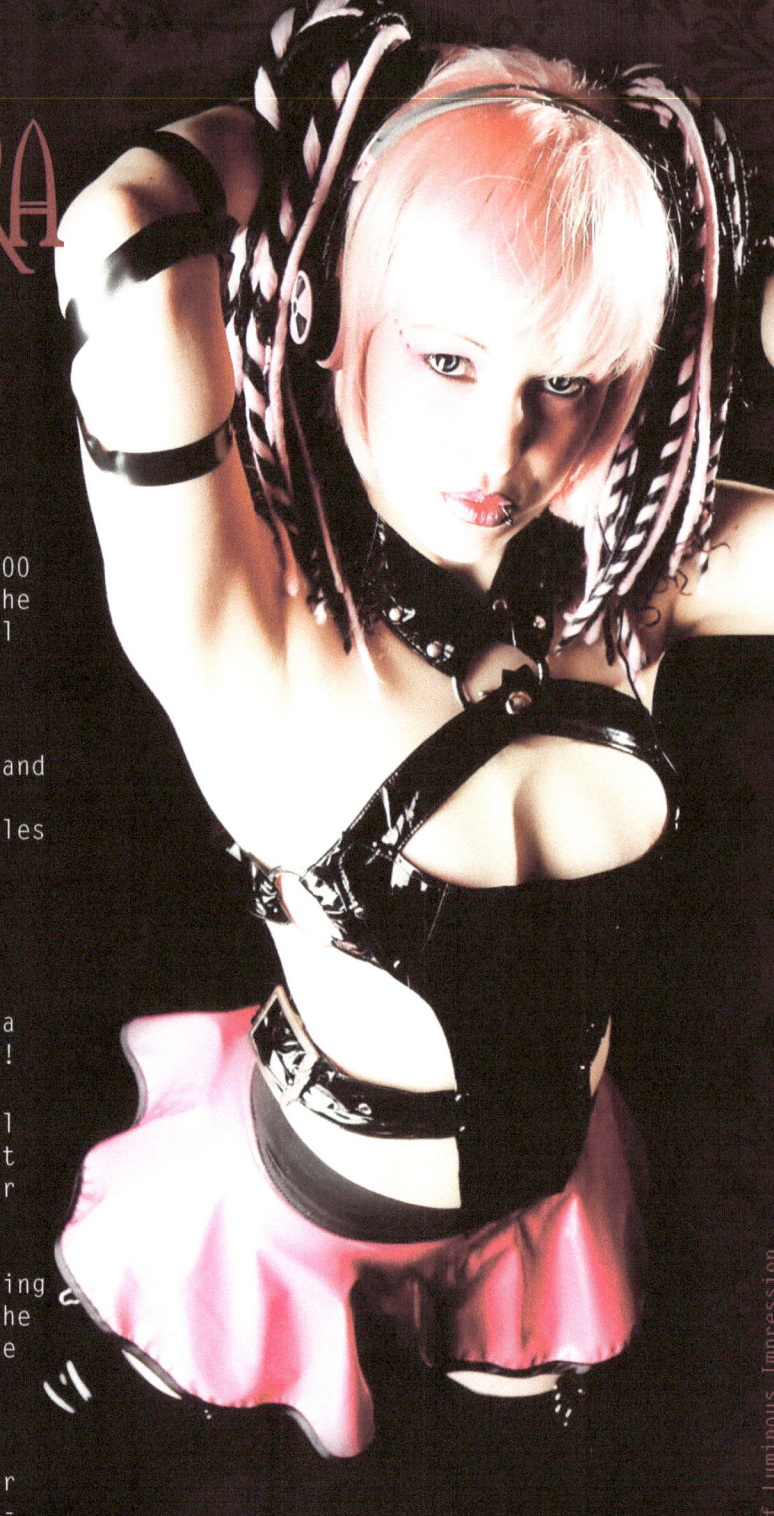

STILL

GRAVEYARDGIRL: AMARA

This Walking, Talking, Posing, Picture Snapping, Performing Beauty is a virtual "Photo Shoot-In-A-Can"

Also known as the girl of a 1000 faces, Amara is a veteran of the modeling world, with an arsenal of clothes, wigs and shoes to work with.

Amara is a clothing designer, and will soon be launching her own line, focusing on the many styles of Lolita and Japanese Street Fashion, and throwing in some goth and cyber. She claims all the 2+ rooms of clothes (and let's not forget the racks and racks of shoes and wigs) have a purpose... they make her happy!

She is a MUA as well, doing all her own makeup, as well as most of the models who work with her or Mystic.

She has recently started shooting and creating art, too, under the name "Immortal Image" where she is fast becoming known as an excellent shooter and artist.

What else is there left for her to master? She is a Fetish Performer and Dancer with SingleCell Productions, A Model - Graveyard Girl, Asylum Girl, ex-SG Girl, Amara Suicide, Clothing Designer, Photographer and Artist... only time will tell.

photo: © Jimmy C of Luminous Impression

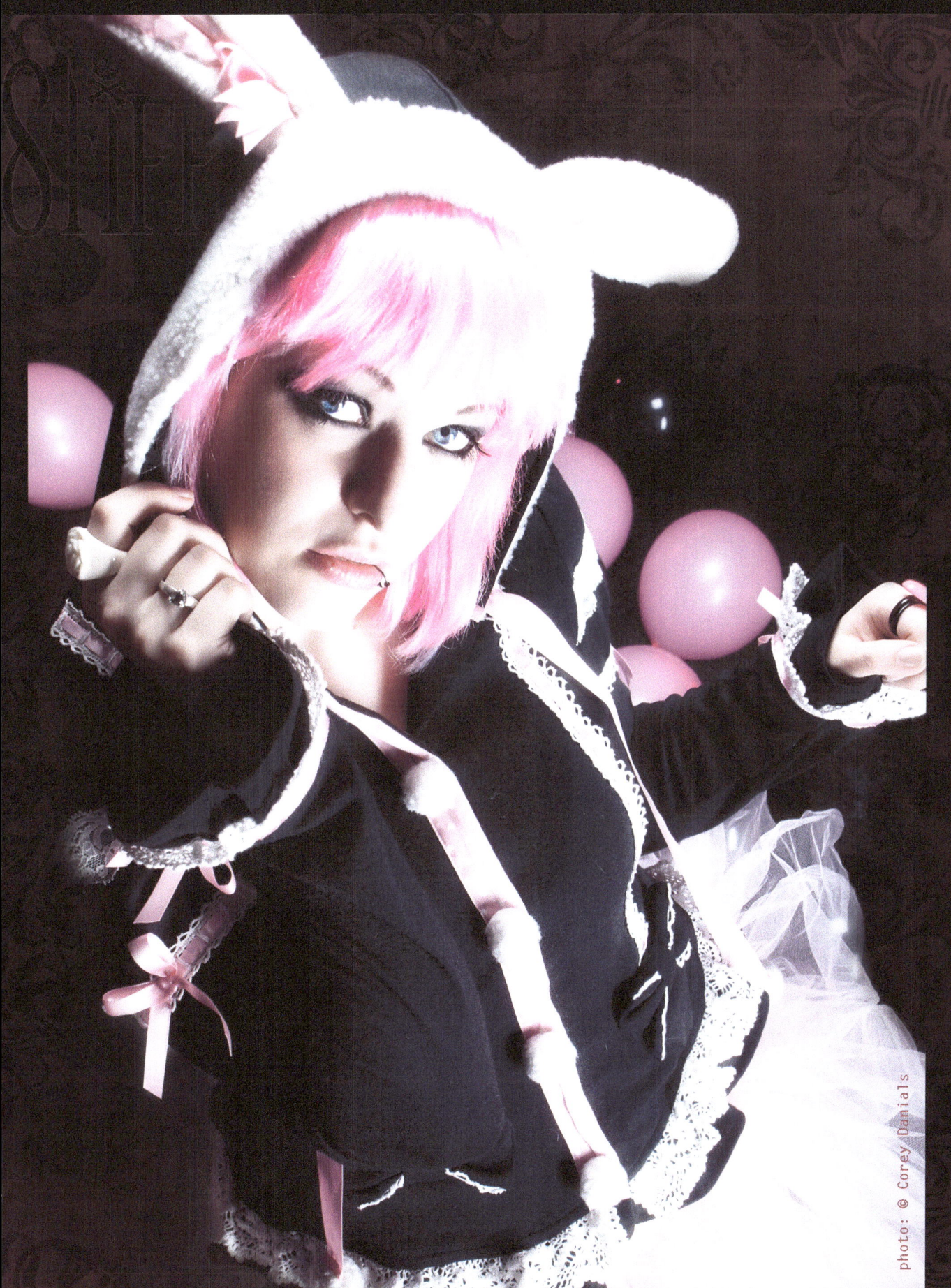

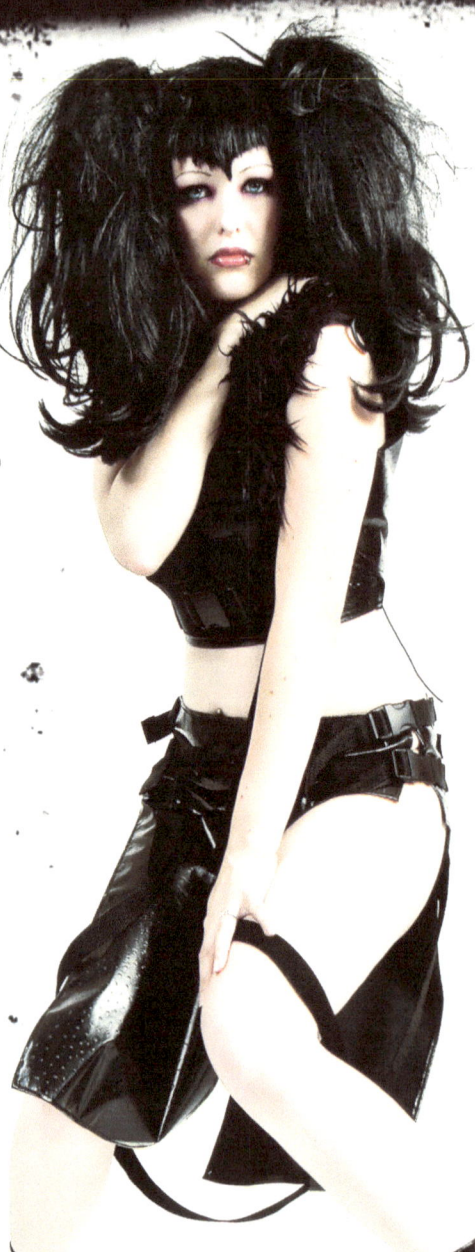

STIFF

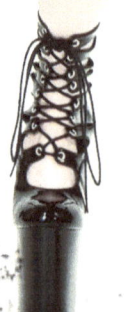

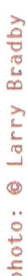

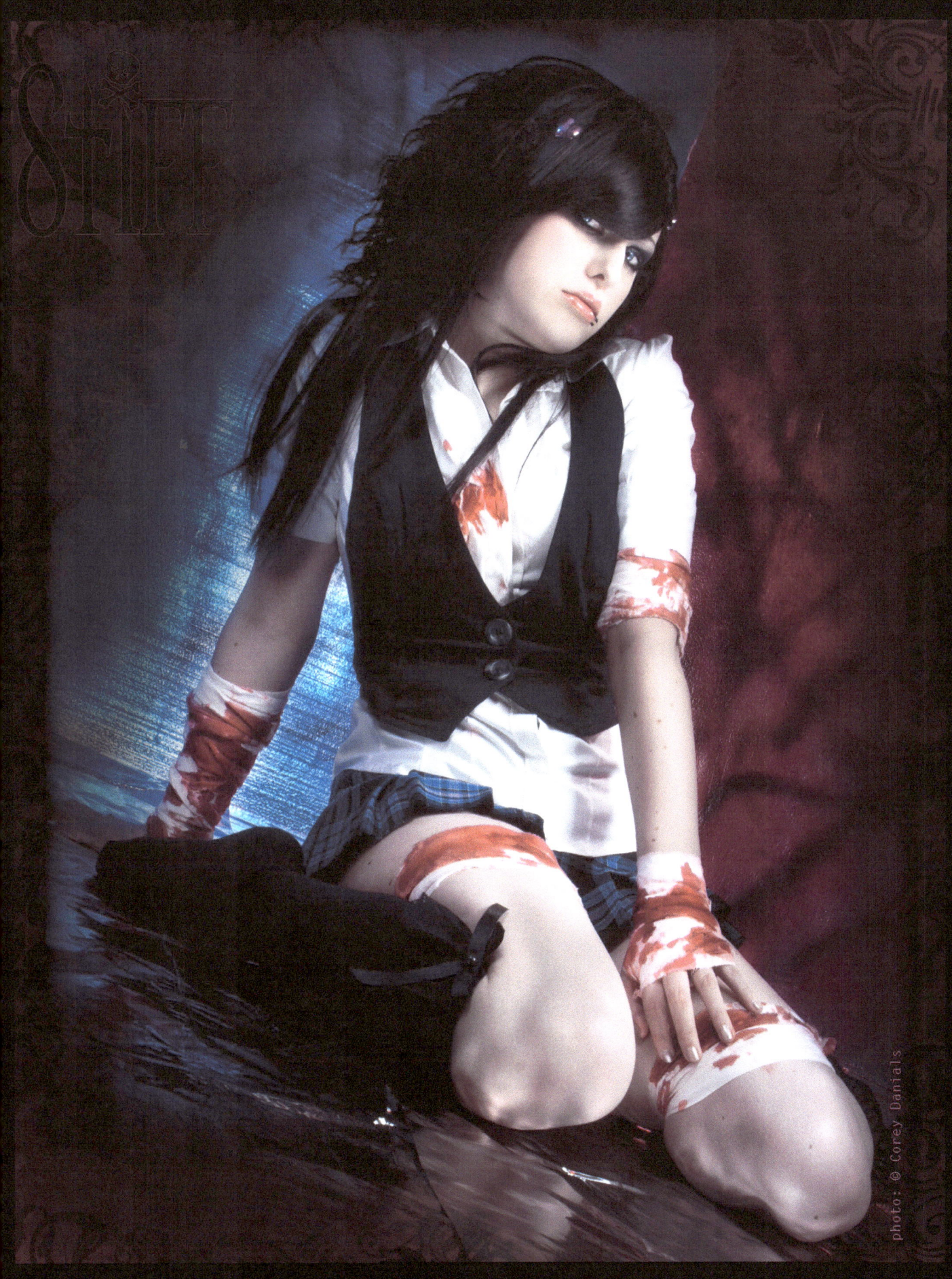

STIFF

photo: © Corey Danials

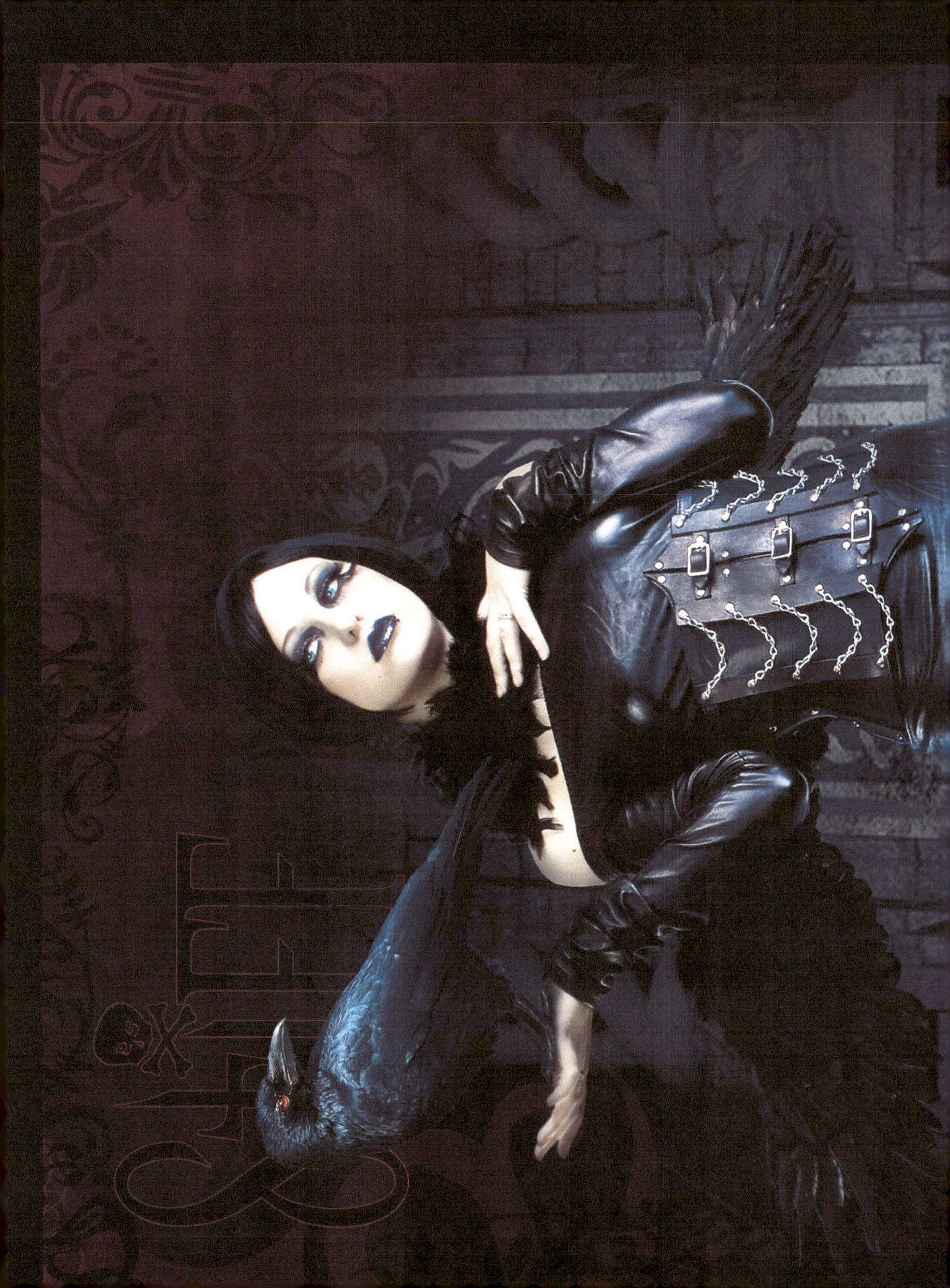

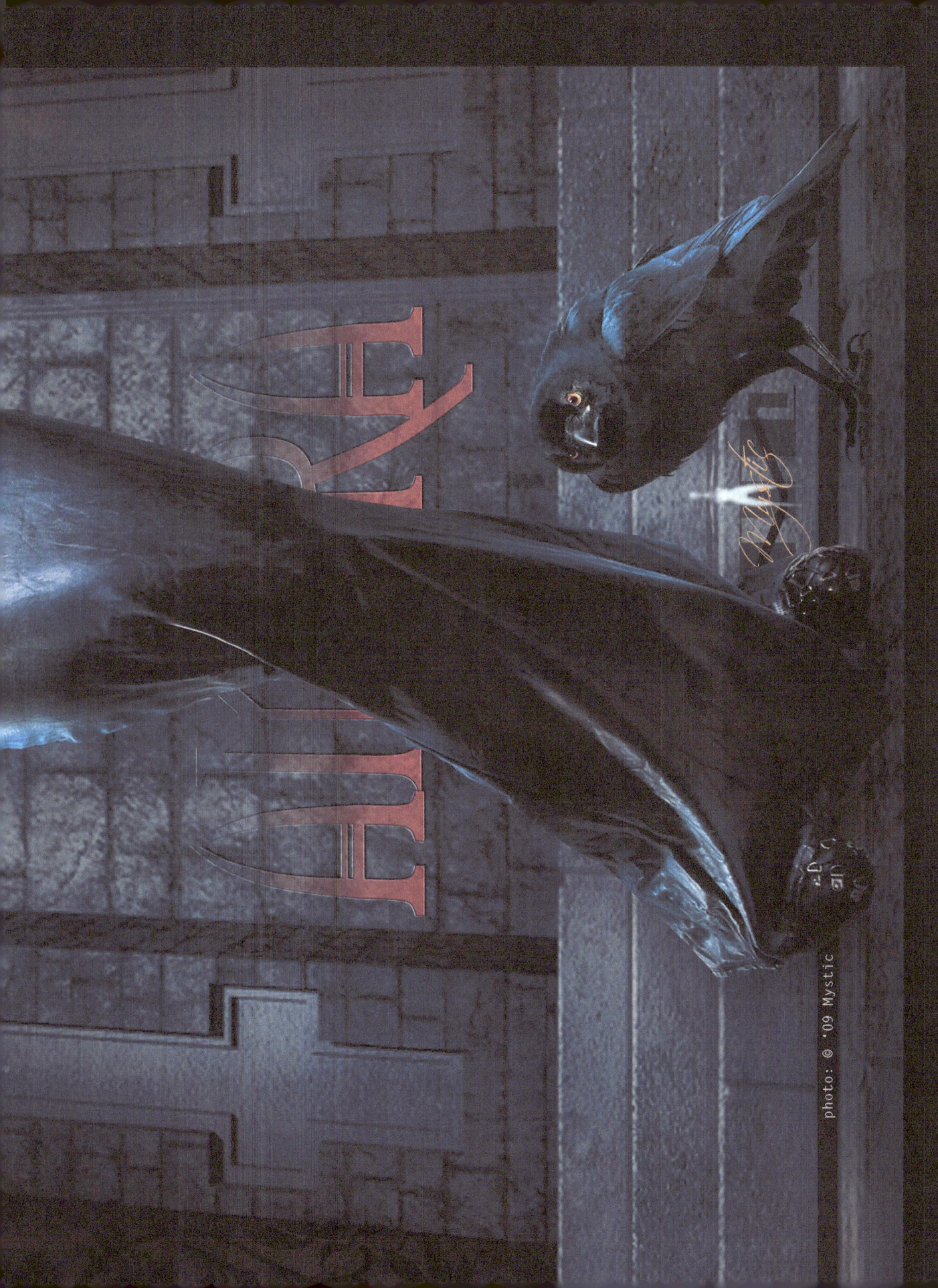

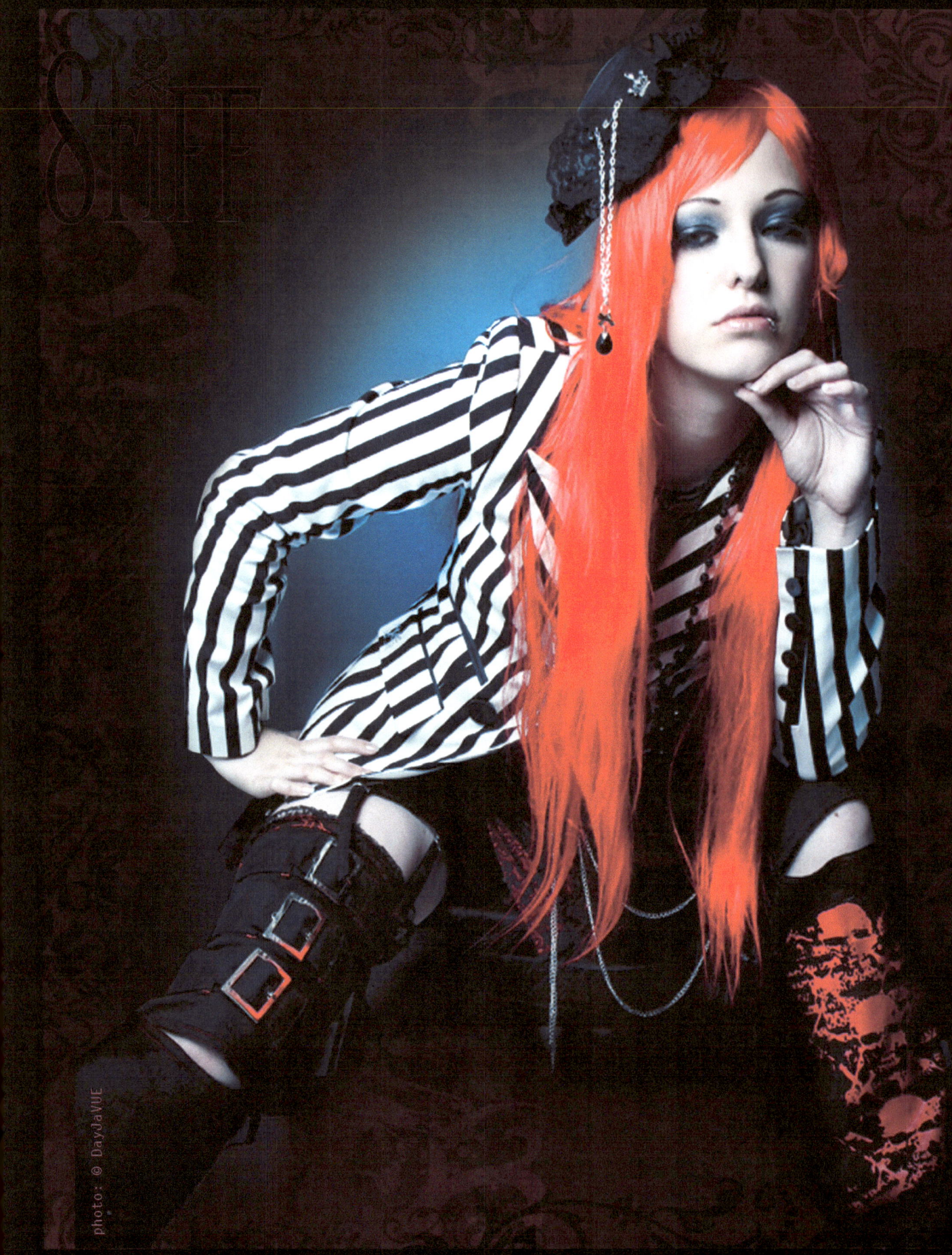

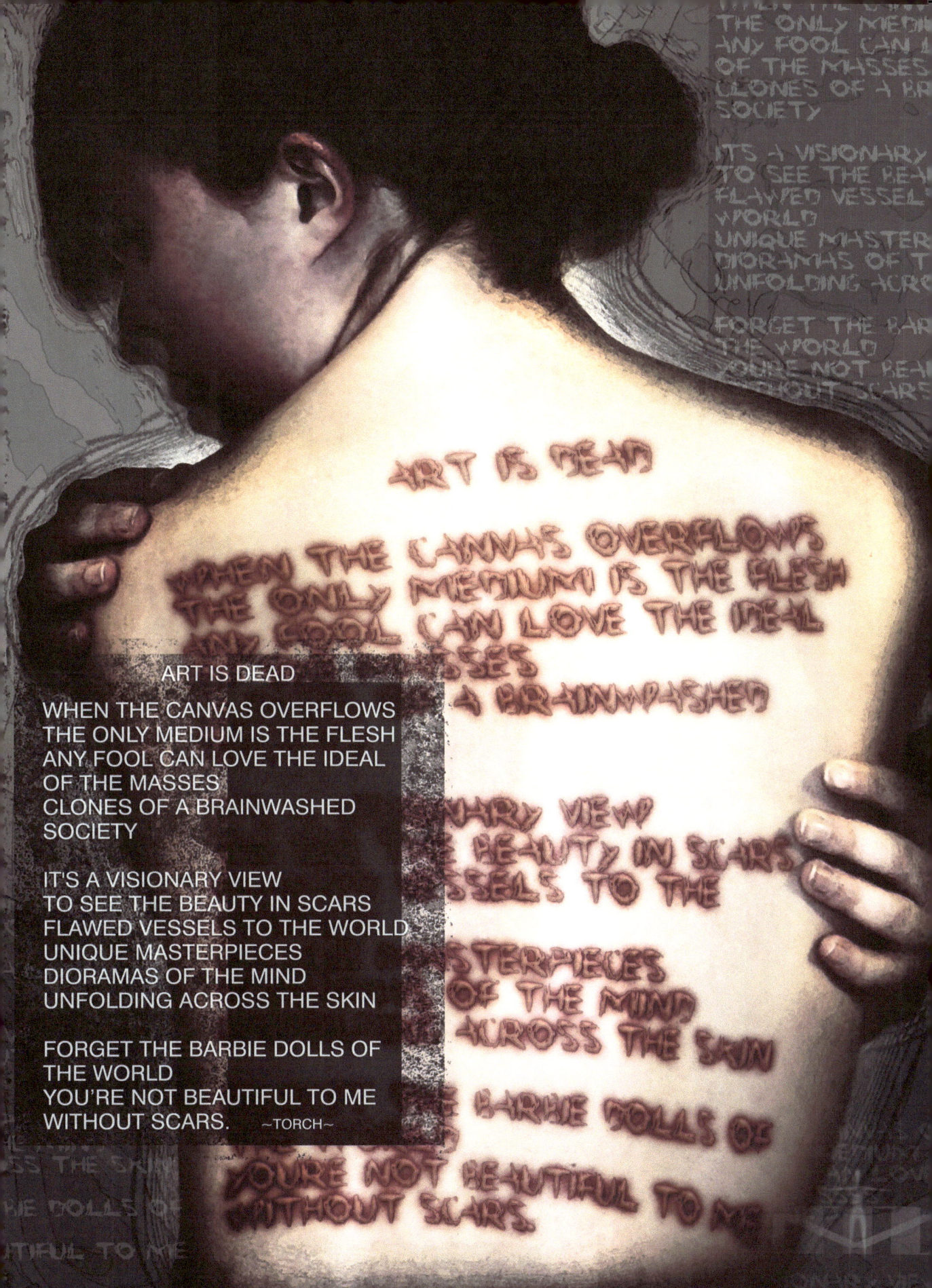

ART IS DEAD

WHEN THE CANVAS OVERFLOWS
THE ONLY MEDIUM IS THE FLESH
ANY FOOL CAN LOVE THE IDEAL
OF THE MASSES
CLONES OF A BRAINWASHED
SOCIETY

IT'S A VISIONARY VIEW
TO SEE THE BEAUTY IN SCARS
FLAWED VESSELS TO THE WORLD
UNIQUE MASTERPIECES
DIORAMAS OF THE MIND
UNFOLDING ACROSS THE SKIN

FORGET THE BARBIE DOLLS OF
THE WORLD
YOU'RE NOT BEAUTIFUL TO ME
WITHOUT SCARS.   ~TORCH~

The Crow, The Moon and Falling Darkness ~Sym

He sits,
draped over the chair.
Leg cocked over the arm.
Barely breathing,
silent subtle rises give way
to the acknowledgment of his birth.

The occasional twist of his finger,
movement of his neck
arch of his hip,
sends the sound of aged leather
and steel armor
ricocheting warmly across the stone walls of the turret.
He has long taken on the look of falling darkness.

Black feathers scatter
suddenly,
as a murder of crows flood in through the stone windows.
He calls to them with his sullenness.
Satirical eyes wild with the envy of their flight.

He can control them,
could grasp his long white fingers,
tightening his grip,
in a moment
any one of them would fall to the ground.

Sadness wraps him with the thought.
He would not hurt a single piece of down
on a single one of his beloved birds.
He loves them,
croons them,
protects them.
In payment they do his bidding.
Leaving the great castle tower
collecting his souls.

Souls that line shelves,
shelves that line walls
walls that stretch forever.

The souls almost please him,
he watches them spin
and turn about in each jar.
Small ones, dark ones,
light ones and large ones.
They never stare back,
they never judge,
they just are.
Are there,
in his jars, under his thumb, in his absence of light.

Then one day the crows returned
with only one soul for his jars.
He was angry and resentful
sent them off once more.
The only bird left held steadfast
to the solitary soul,
arching its neck to its Master.
Offering its prize at his feet.
He reached for a jar,
uncapped its prison,
reached out,
he sealed the soul.

But just as he did,
there was a sound.
Whirling around to the window,
then back to the bird,

"Who goes there?"

Silence abounds,
nothing but the wind was heard.

"Show yourself" he bellowed.
And nothing still.

The jar became warm in his hands,
and then warmer still.
Until the heat was no longer bearable
and his long fingers
let go of their clutch.

To the ground the jar sailed,
in a sudden instant
the explosion of glass was deafening.
The soul flooded out into the room,
growing larger at first
a liquid and then a solid.
In a few short moments of confusion,
he was looking at a woman.

Warmth for his cold,
smile for his sadness,
kisses for his pain.
She reached up
and took his face within her hands,
she showed no fear at the depth of his well,

Leaning in she began rubbing her cheek along his chin.
She stood breathing in his smell
from the curve of his long neck,
standing on her toes,
with him still in confusion.
She laid her lips on his nose.
Slid her mouth across his eyes
and laid to a stop at his ear,
whispered.

"You are more beautiful,
you are stronger,
you are more important
than all the grains of sand
holding all the drops in the ocean.
If allowed
I would lay sleeping with you,
joined by only skin
lit only by the glow of the moon".

Breathing out,
he opened his eyes,
and she was gone.
Leaving only the smell of her skin
The warmth of her hands
The fissure in his heart.

Taking two long steps he reached the window.
Dawn was coming,
but he could still see her moon

Roll me   ~Sym

Roll me
Out in the puddles created from the tears of my dragons
Lay your hands upon the fleshy parts of my thigh
Can you feel the fire that burns through my bones leaving them hollow?
The flames are controlled
Just under the skin

Roll me
In the soil turned freshly for my own grave
The black gold smells of fermented hooves
The remnant entrails of the four horsemen
Worms and maggots sign my place card

Roll me
Over the stones the great ships collide with
Breaking steel like buttons of butterscotch
Smashed on a lighted glass floor
Here the shadows cannot hide

Roll me
Under your tongue
Slide me over the teeth in which bite the lips of many
I know what you are
I can smell it on your breathe
Every time you steal a trinket of some ones soul
It leaves its mark for me to find

ASK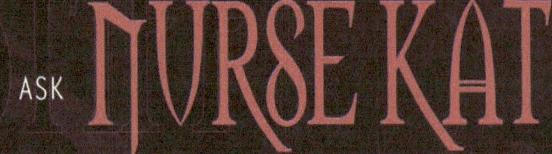

NURSE KAT

A little bit about Nurse Kat Kalashnikov:

Fetish performer/model, artist, clothing designer, and constant tank girl. Performed up and down the East Coast, featured in national magazines, and crash landing at an event near you!

Number of tattoos: countless.

Number of piercings: depends on how many needles she can stick in herself at one time.

Loves: blood and alcohol(together or separated), chains, rivetheads, medical supplies, latex, and power tools for all the wrong reasons.

Hates: people with bedtimes, low-grade alcohol, and patients that don't scream...

STUDIOS

Q: I woke up still drunk after the show. Does that count as a hangover?

drunkdude81

A: Not at all. Just throw on some sunglasses, pretend that sun is a slightly brighter moon, and get back to drinking. The party doesn't stop just because you passed out for a few hours. And don't worry ladies, bars are indoors so you won't lose your corpse-beauty pale skin.

Q: I've caught 2 of your shows on the road. Do you have a favorite city to perform in?

moshpitqueeny

A: Every city is like a new experience, I love having a new crowd to perform for. At the same time I love performing at a hometown, and seeing some faces in the crowd that already know how crazy I am (for the other cities its still a pleasant surprise!).

Q: What does gutter glam mean?

glamcurious

A: Its spilling wine on your perfect dress, so splashing the rest of the bottle on it and calling it DIY. Its saying hey we are out of beer and nowhere is open to serve us some, so you fly to the nearest city that is. Its being high class gutter trash, the new brand of rock star that knows they are scum and is out to make it fashionable.

Q: Any advice for a someone trying to break into modeling/performance?

dgenirate

A: Get yourself out there. Network, network, network. Every show, concert, event, even wine tasting is a way to promote yourself. Make an image and show it. Set up web sites (there are plenty of model sites to join), search for local photographers/ fetish companies (if looking to perform) and research what it is you want to do. I hang up mirrors in every room of the house so I know how I pose and look on stage. I read S&M introduction books so I can properly prepare myself to perform.

TECH FROM THE CRYPT

The Jaunty Jackelope
aka Ubuntu version 9.x   ~Antigone Kilma

In my opinion, there's a better OS for PC. Ubuntu Linux, that cute little penguin guy. A lot of friends said not to take the plunge, but being a tad strong-willed, I did anyway. And I am soooo not looking back!

In seven months, I haven't had a single hardware conflict, virus, or spyware. Everything I've attached worked right when plugged in. And believe me, I've tried all kinds of off-the-wall stuff. Even plugged in a four year old Kodak all-in-one, waited a few minutes, and voila! I could scan, print, and fax immediately. All I had to do was confirm the specific model number. No discs, no "if this, then that", nothin'. Its all just handled, and handled well.

In a similar seven month time frame, I had over 100 viruses, a 1,000 spyware gizmos, and had to re-install the OS 3-4 times. You could say I tend to push my systems to their limits. Which means if its safe and stable for me, it probably is for just about anyone.

Did I mention it's free?

Why? Because it's Linux, which is "open source" and open source (usually) means free, and if any nerd anywhere on Earth wants to use the same or similar piece of hardware, then they write the program and submit it to the operating system. Done deal. If another geek makes improvements, they then write and submit the updates. Tada!

And if a hacker wants in, we all know about it and sic rabid hyenas on them in their sleep. I don't have firewall, anti-virus, or anti-spyware programs of any kind installed. The core "brain" of Ubuntu is so well written and protected, there's just no need for them.

What about software? You can use Firefox for your browser, just like you do now. Or Epiphany looks and feels similar to IE, except that it actually works. Same for Office software. I use Open Office (www.openoffice.org) that reads & writes most Microsoft Office file formats for easy collaboration. And this is true for almost anything you wanna do.

For newbies, I suggest going to www.ubuntu.com and ordering the CD & manual to get started. If you're techie enough to be dangerous, download and install the dual-boot files (also on ubuntu.com). If you don't like it, Ubuntu will gracefully bow out. But if you're a cool kid, you'll get the CD, back up your data, have the restoration disks (just in case), and start over.

You'll be happy you did. It's faster, more reliable, prettier, and friendlier, and there are thousands of folks around the world happy to help you at any time. We're a friendly group, open to newbies and converts. Guess you could say we're "open source", too.

Left4Dead 2: The Zombie Apocalypse Continues
By: Michael Mendoza

We all know that last year an ambitious game took everything we thought we knew about the growing zombie threat and turned it on its head. The original Left4Dead brought not only fast-moving super zombies, but gave them even greater superpowers (the game calls them "Special Infected") the likes of which no undead should have any sense having (not that it wasn't entertaining, mind you).

Well, the programmers and creative team at Valve have done it again, and this time with renewed pizzazz.

Left4Dead 2 has flown off the shelves since its release not one month prior to this review. Featuring new campaign maps, weapons (both firearms and melee), better survivor and enemy A.I., and new game modes to make even veteran L4D1 players feel the pressure, we've been given the special privilege to feel the tension of the zombie apocalypse in an all new and ever more horrifying way.

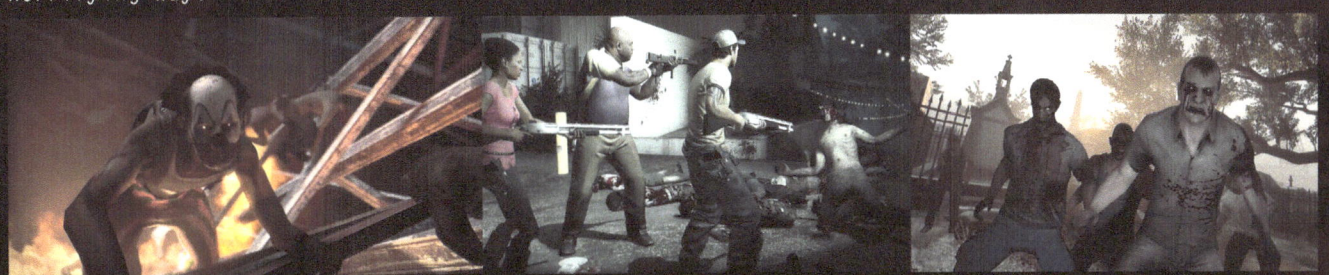

The limited game play map that was provided in L4D1 has been upgraded to several new and expansive campaign levels, each of which provides its own backstory through the not-so-subtle piles of corpses that others have left behind as they attempted to survive, and each level flows into the next, weaving the overall campaign into a fluid state that further improves on the brevity of the original. And, of course, the added tension of no campaign being the same, as zombie placements and ambushes change from play through to play through and depending on how well you're doing, helps to ensure greater and greater re-playability.

Another definite improvement can be found in the game's A.I. which, while not perfected, has taken a few leaps forward in comparison to the original's. Your fellow survivors in single player mode offer more intelligent maneuvers and tactics, and seem to follow your example a little better in some instances rather than run out on their own. However, improved A.I. does come with a price, as your enemies are benefiting from those improvements as well and, with the new special powers that the undead have been granted (controlling your characters movement, spewing pools of acid, and hitting you like a tanker truck just to mention a few), you'll have to pull out all the stops just to make it to the next checkpoint.

Of course, the benefits of all these upgrades to enemies can be had by players as well, as L4D2 continues to offer the versus play option, allowing players to completely turn against survivors and enjoy the wicked benefits of being one of the undead themselves. With the new level designs, this offers a whole new way to completely devastate players just when they thought they'd reached a safe point, and survivors themselves will reap the benefits of the new firearms (making their enemies resemble swiss cheese rather than the undead) and the highly enjoyable melee weapons (limbs flying through the air... beautiful!) to teach their would-be destroyers rethink their strategies time and again. Prior to the game's release, anyone who pre-ordered L4D2 from Gamestop stores was given an exclusive code for a baseball bat.

And for those players who think they've got the game play figured out? Try the new Realism mode, where you get no special indication of the location of your fellow survivors, of in-game aids like ammo or health items, where you could find yourself completely alone with no one to help you and no way to find them, and enjoy your final moments as the zombie horde overwhelms you. Tense enough for you yet? Didn't think so.

Overall, Left4Dead 2 doesn't truly break any ground as a game from the original but, that said, it still offers vast upgrades over the systems that made the game so horrifyingly wonderful in the first place. With new game play features, weapons, improved A.I. and an amplified level of tension to boot, Left4Dead 2 has raised the bar on what we should expect from survival-horror games.

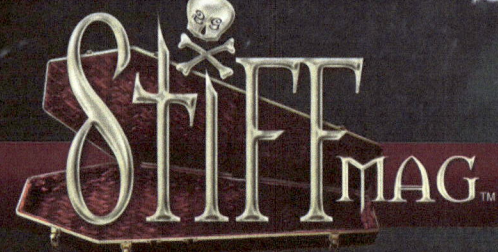

Genitorturers
Fall 2009 Tour
Spartanburg, SC

Photo © '09 Billy Liner

Graveyard Boulevard
2009 Fatality Ball
Charlotte, NC

STIFF MAG™

Photo © '09 Billy Liner

GRAVEYARDGIRL: VIVICA

Vivica Hallow has a bad habit of setting people on fire. On purpose.

She is a multi-talented touring stage performer, clothing designer and model, touring throughout the East coast and bringing a unique blend of mayhem, destruction and attitude to the stages and runways of a city near you.

Home based with SingleCell Productions in Charlotte NC, she can often be found dreaming up new ways to bring fire acts to the stage or new pathways to pain and pleasure.

If she asks you for a light...

RUN!

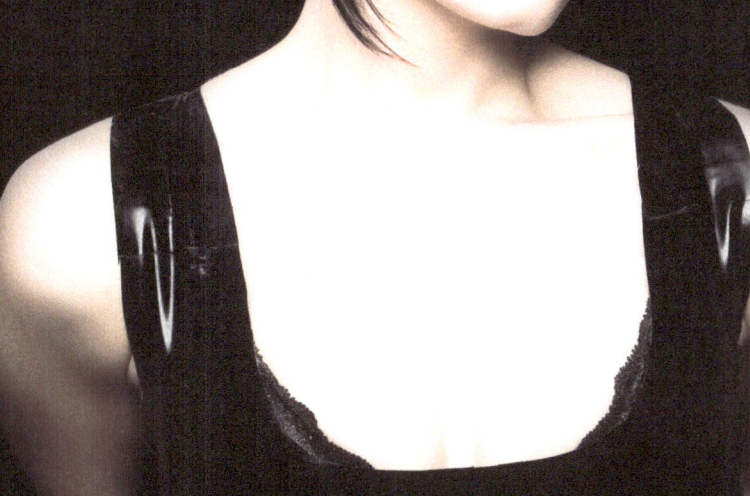

STIFF

studios

photo: © Justin Kates

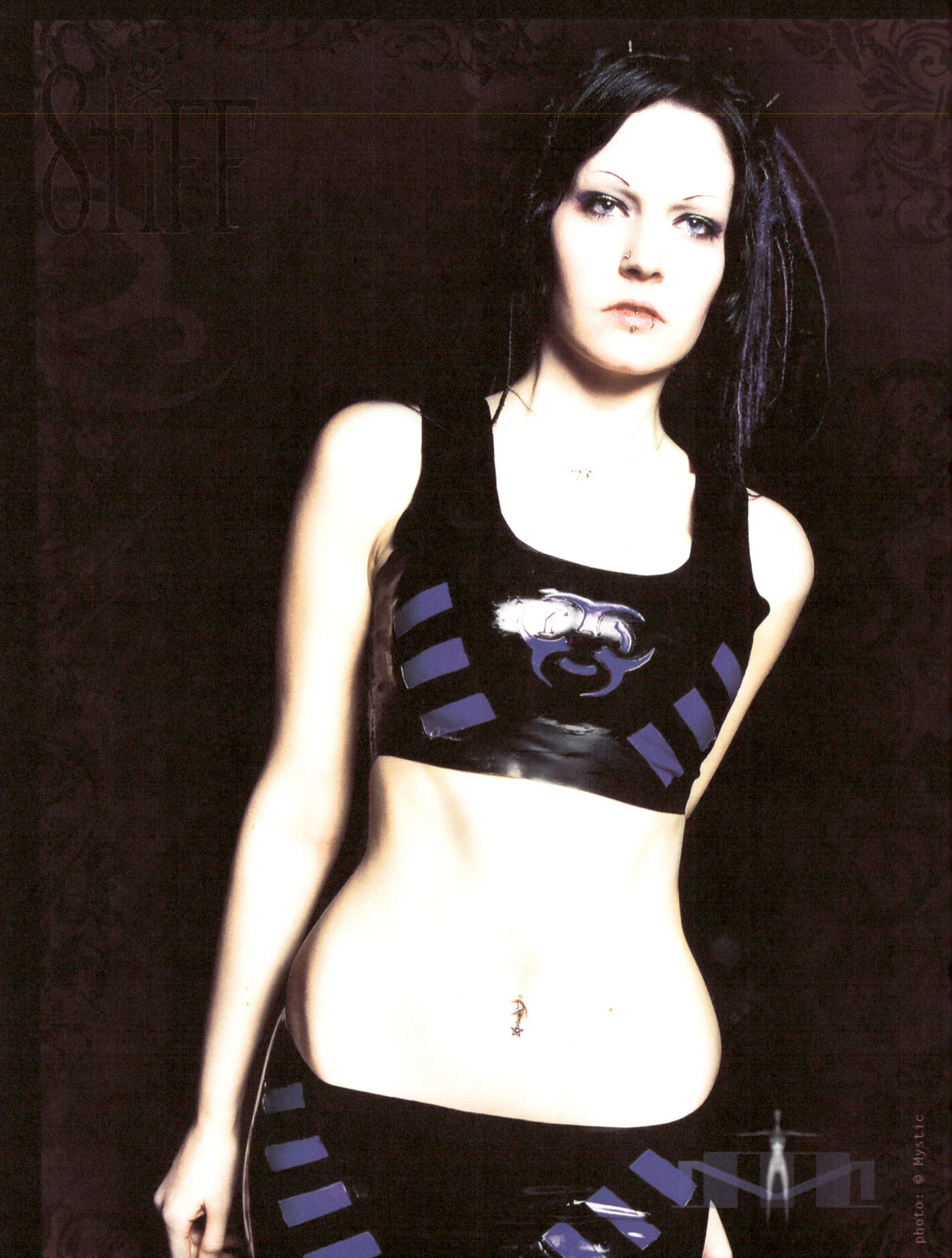

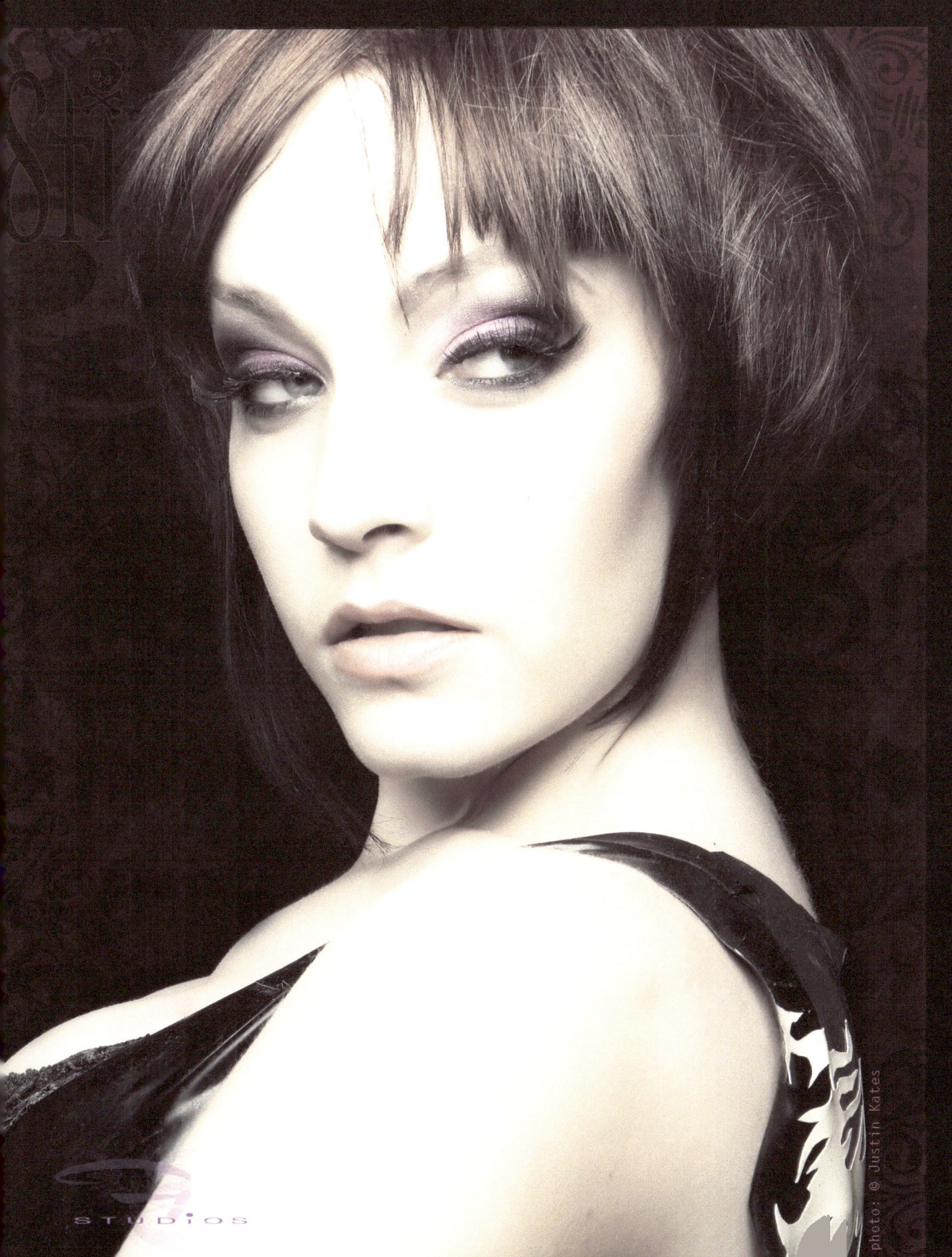

RETRO REVIEW

The Last Man On Earth
Vincent Price - 1964

DO YOU DARE IMAGINE WHAT IT WOULD BE LIKE TO BE THE LAST MAN ON EARTH...OR THE LAST WOMAN?
Alive among the lifeless...alone among the crawling creatures of evil that make the night hideous with their inhuman craving!

VINCENT PRICE STARRING AS

THE LAST Man on Earth

FRANCA BETTOIA · EMMA DANIELI · GIACOMO ROSSI STUART · Directed by SIDNEY SALKOW · Produced by ROBERT L. LIPPERT
Screenplay by LOGAN SWANSON and WILLIAM F. LEICESTER · Based on a novel by RICHARD MATHESON · AN AMERICAN INTERNATIONAL PICTURE

After such a huge success (in both box office and DVD/BluRay sales) with "I Am Legend", a popular science fiction horror film starring Will Smith and based on a novel by Richard Matheson, we thought we'd let Hollywood keep all the modern hype on yet another remake and instead, give some credit to the original for once! So here's your Retro-Review kiddies...

"The Last Man On Earth"!

Now, for those keeping score, that's three adaptations for Matheson's novel, the last being 1971's "The Omega Man", which starred Charlton Heston. But of course, the book was first adapted for the 1964 film "The Last Man On Earth", a bleak post-apocalyptic nightmare starring Vincent Price. While still taking a few liberties with the source material, the Price film is easily the more faithful of the two, and this Italian/British coproduction has been considered a cult classic, as well as a personal favorite for years. The film opens with a series of shots depicting a city with no citizens. A few bodies lie here and there, but otherwise the streets are empty. The Marquee in front of a church reads "The End Has Come." The camera moves into a residential neighborhood and into the home of Dr. Robert Morgan (Price), the titular last man on earth whose sanity is hanging by a thread. Each night Morgan's house is assaulted by vampire-like creatures, the after effects of the global plague that has wiped out mankind. The creatures are bloodthirsty but weak and are only dangerous in numbers.

Morgan awakens and begins going through his daily routine. The garlic on the door must be replaced as well as the shattered mirror (the creatures can't stand their own reflections), there are bodies to be disposed of as the creatures feed on their own, and of course there are wooden stakes to be made. He gases up his car and sets about his new vocation, methodically exploring every building in the city and driving a stake through the heart of any of the creatures he comes across.

The film takes place in 1968 and we learn through an extended flashback that society fell three years before that. Morgan worked as a research scientist with his friend Ben Cortman (Giacomo Rossi-Stuart, star of many an Italian genre film, most notably Mario Bava's "Kill Baby Kill"), not realizing that Cortman would one day be one of the creatures pounding on Morgan's door every night. A highly contagious disease "carried by the wind" has migrated from Europe and decimated the population of the world. Morgan doesn't believe Cortman when he repeats rumors that some of those killed by the plague have been returning to life. When Morgan's wife Virginia (Emma Danieli) succumbs to the plague and he can not bear the thought of her being incinerated with all the others he buries her in secret. The scene in which she returns to him, still wearing the dirty house coat in which she was buried and with choral singers screeching on the sound track, is an old school marrow-chiller.

Morgan's solitude shows signs of easing
when a dog shows up on his doorstep, and
one day while going about his business he
meets a woman named Ruth (Franca Bettoia)
whose presence in the daylight proves she
is not one of the creatures. Things are not
as they seem, though, and as the poster for
the Will Smith version of this story pro-
claims, "the last man on earth is not

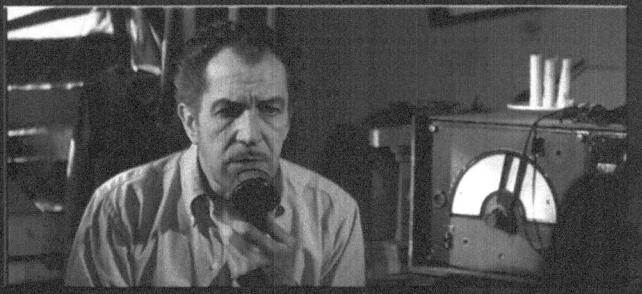

It just ain't a Vincent Price movie until some scenery gets chewed,but Price's talent
for going over the top serves him well when Morgan is on the verge of slipping into
madness. There are some wonderfully haunting moments like the time shift from Morgan's
daughter's birthday party to a point some time later after the plague has struck. We
shift from a backyard scene of children playing to the same yard but empty now and
with a howling wind tearing through it. George Romero has stated many times how "Night
of the Living Dead" was inspired by Matheson's novel, but after seeing Cortland and
the other creatures pounding on the exterior of Morgan's house, the similarity to
Romero's first film is obvious and I have to imagine he saw "Last Man on Earth" as
well.

Be especially cautious when shopping for this flick on DVD. The film has long since
fallen into the public domain, so pretty much anyone can release it. There was a "Last
Man on Earth/House on Haunted Hill" double feature DVD around some time ago, but it
was
a grainy low contrast pan and scan print of the American International Television version which is so bad it's practically un-watchable. There is a pretty good release out
from Madacy Home Video which features a wide screen print with surprisingly good quality picture and sound. An even better copy is available as part of MGM's "Midnight
Movies" line, paired up for a double feature with another apocalyptic movie from the
period, "Panic
in Year Zero".

Sadly, the film rarely gets the credit it deserves for being one of the earliest
"modern" horror movies, often being completely overshadowed by the much more flamboy-
ant "Omega Man" of ten years later. But if nothing else, the shameless Hollywood re-
remake of the film that occurred with "I Am Legend" should draw even more attention to
this overlooked 1960s gem. So, when you're out and about looking for a good classic
horror flick for a dark night in, pick up a copy of this one, it's not only a good
buy, but undoubtedly an insanely cheap one!

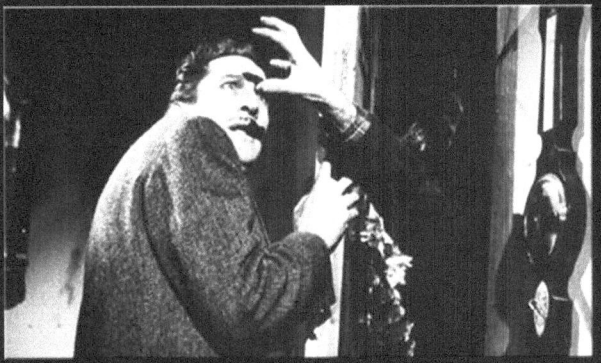

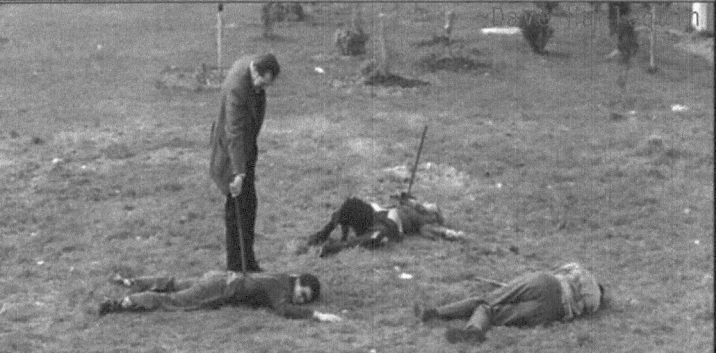

FRIDAY - JANUARY 22 - 2010

DAMMIT JANET
3746 N. DAVIDSON ST
CHARLOTTE NC

$10
9PM-2AM
18+

SCI.x
SINGLE CELL INDUSTRIAL
THE SOUND OF QUEEN CITY'S UNDERGROUND

END-THE-DJ ///// MIXTRESS KRIKETT
AND SPECIAL GUESTS
FOURTH FRIDAYS @ DAMMIT JANET

The New SOUND of the *Queen City's* UNDERGROUND

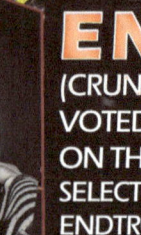

END: THE DJ
(CRUNCH POD, KOMOR KOMMANDO)
VOTED THE #1 INDUSTRIAL CLUB DJ
ON THE DJ LIST, END WILL BE PLAYING
SELECTED TRACKS FROM HIS NEW ALBUM
ENDTROVERT OUT IN FEBRUARY
ON CRUNCH POD MUSIC

MIXTRESS KRIKETT
(SINGLE CELL PRODUCTIONS)
CHARLOTTE'S SINISTER SPINSTRESS
OF DARK DANCE MUSIC

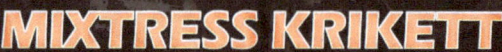

& SPECIAL GUESTS

DJ AEROS

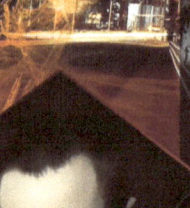
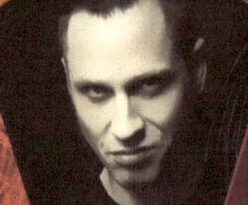
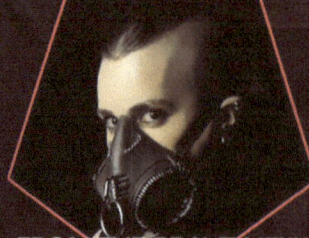
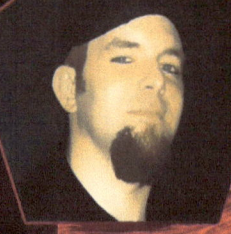

M1KILL
SPECIAL DJ SET FROM THE
FRONTMAN OF ANGELS ON ACID

FROM THE BRAVE NEW
WORLD NIGHT IN
KNOXVILLE, TENNESSEE

DJ POE
AN EXPERT DJ FROM
CHICAGO & RALEIGH NC

FEAT. SINGLECELL GOGO-DANCERS & FALLOUT FASHION CYBER ACCESSORIES

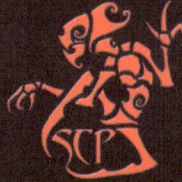
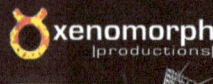
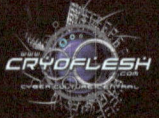
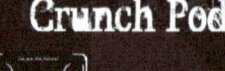
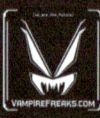

xenomorph [productions]

CRYOFLESH

DAMMIT JANET!

RE:GEN MAGAZINE

Crunch Pod

VAMPIREFREAKS.COM

BPM TALENT